Praise for

E P I P H A N Y

"Chuck Smith jr. gives us a refresher course on how to masterfully handle the wonderful Word of God. I recommend this book!"
>—GREG LAURIE, senior pastor of Harvest Christian Fellowship and author of *Why Believe?* and *The Upside Down Church*

"If you 'want to want to study the Bible,' buy this book. But for people who already love God's Word, *Epiphany* is not a book you buy; it's a book you master."
>—LEONARD SWEET, Drew Theological School, George Fox University

"As usual, Chuck's work reeks of Christ's glory and kingdom."
>—SCOTTY SMITH, senior pastor of Christ Community Church, Franklin, Tennessee

"I love Chuck's enthusiasm to hear God's voice for ourselves in fresh ways."
>—KENTON BESHORE, senior pastor of Mariners Church

"This book doesn't tell people *what* to think about the Bible but rather helps people learn *how* to engage with the Bible wisely, humbly, personally, and fruitfully."
>—BRIAN MCLAREN, pastor and author of *A New Kind of Christian* and *Finding Faith*

"If you want to reapproach the Scriptures with a renewed hunger and a fresh perspective, you *must* read this book."
>—DAN KIMBALL, author of *The Emerging Church: Vintage Christianity for New Generations* and founding pastor of Graceland at Santa Cruz Bible Church

"*Epiphany* is a gold mine for the individual reader and the study group leader and a refreshing read for the 'tired expert.'"

—REV. DR. MAGGI DAWN, author and theologian, King's College, Cambridge

"Discover the delight of an insight-filled book written by a skill-filled friend of the Bible."

—TODD HUNTER, director of Allelon Church Planting Foundation and former director of Vineyard-USA

"*Epiphany* sends us back to the Bible with our senses newly sharpened, ready for discoveries even in the most familiar places."

—ANDY CROUCH, editor-in-chief of *re:generation quarterly*

"Chuck Smith jr. makes what many consider to be a dry subject come alive. I found myself smiling as a renewed hunger developed to see my own Bible reading transformed."

—SKIP HEITZIG, pastor and author of *How to Study the Bible and Enjoy It*

"*Epiphany* will guide you in a very practical way to an understanding of the Bible. Jesus compares the Bible to seed planted in various types of soil. The seed that fell on good soil was the person who heard the Word and understood it. Reading the Bible is important, but *understanding* what you have read is even more important."

—CHUCK SMITH SR., senior pastor, Calvary Chapel of Costa Mesa

EPIPHANY

EPIPHANY

DISCOVER THE DELIGHT OF GOD'S WORD

CHUCK SMITH, JR.

WATERBROOK
PRESS

EPIPHANY
PUBLISHED BY WATERBROOK PRESS
2375 Telstar Drive, Suite 160
Colorado Springs, Colorado 80920
A division of Random House, Inc.

ISBN 1-57856-542-1

Library of Congress Cataloging-in-Publication Data
Smith, Chuck, Jr.
  Epiphany : discover the delight of God's word / Chuck Smith, Jr.—1st ed.
    p. cm.
  ISBN 1-57856-542-1
  1. Bible—Hermeneutics. I. Title.
  BS476 .S66 2003
  220.6'01—dc21

                                                    2002151178

Printed in the United States of America
2003—First Edition

10 9 8 7 6 5 4 3 2 1

Contents

A NEW LOOK AT THE OLD, OLD STORY

Finding Fresh Meaning in the Ancient Narrative

I was driving south (creeping, actually) on the 405 Freeway, trying to remain calm in the Southern California gridlock. The voice of megachurch pastor Greg Laurie boomed from my radio, explaining why there are so many translations of the Bible. Then he made a side comment regarding *The Living Bible:* "My wife and I have a *Living Bible*," he said. "We keep it in a cage."

Sitting alone in my car, I laughed out loud. I imagined Greg and Cathe keeping their Bible inside a locked enclosure so it wouldn't bite anyone. I could hear it growl whenever someone came to the door or walked too near its corner of the room. If you think about it, a *living* Bible certainly would demand more respect than the legions of inert Bibles collecting dust on our bookshelves.

The Bible in any version or translation is "living" and "active" and "sharper than any double-edged sword" (Hebrews 4:12). Reading the Bible can be a dangerous activity, upsetting the balance of your life, ripping apart your cherished ideas, reorganizing your whole world. But reading the Bible can also be calming and reassuring, comforting through grief, healing through depression, and inspiring you toward greatness.

Here's the truth: It's possible to develop a passionate love for the Bible, to pick it up with such eager anticipation that it eclipses your other favorite pursuits in life. It is possible to have such a strong desire to read the Bible that you would rather open the Scriptures than surf the Internet, go to a movie, or attend a sporting event.

At this point, you might think I'm crazy. Fair enough. After thirty years in the ministry, I know that the majority of Christians do not read the Bible every day. Surveys have revealed that most evangelical Christians don't know Isaac from Esau, nor can they list the Ten Commandments or name the twelve apostles. Our biblical literacy is anemic because we are not drawn to the Bible with irresistible desire. Maybe we have trouble making sense out of the Scriptures. Maybe we fail to grasp the Bible's relevance to our daily concerns. Maybe we keep getting lost in its foreign geography and ancient names. These are legitimate concerns, but if we truly believed that the Bible is God's Word, I don't think we would ever find ourselves being bored with it.

Early in my ministry I had a conversation with a friend that reshaped my thinking about the Scriptures. Guy Gray was studying a variety of theological traditions and pulling straight A's in his last year of Bible college. I mentioned to him a verse from Psalm 119: "Oh, how I love your law! I meditate on it all day long" (verse 97). I said something to the effect, "It doesn't make sense to me that David could love the law." For me, the Old Testament law represented a performance-based system in which people tried to win God's favor through strict compliance to His commandments. It reminded me of the religious legalism that hounded Jesus' steps, that was vigorously opposed by the apostle Paul, and that has seeped into a great many churches today.

Guy saw things completely differently. "It makes perfect sense to me how David could love God's law," he said. "I love the law too; it is beautiful, profound, and rich in spiritual revelation." My friend introduced me to the works of several theologians whose interpretations of the Old Testament uncovered amazing ways that God had revealed Himself. I had listened to solid Bible teaching my entire life, but these new interpreta-tions deepened my love for God. They also energized my desire to gain a better understanding of the Bible. I continue to pursue that goal today, nearly three decades later. This book is an attempt to equip you with the interpretive tools that will lead you to experiencing a new touch from God through deeper exploration of the Scriptures.

In the chapters that follow, we will explore nine methods that will lead you to a clearer understanding of God's message to us. We will also exam-ine some dangers to avoid in interpreting Scripture. I'm confident that as you use these new tools, your eyes will be opened to aspects of God's char-acter that you haven't fully experienced in the past. You will begin a deeper and more authentic process of spiritual growth and development. You will become more faithful in obeying God and honoring Him with your life. And you will find your heart being softened and changed, resulting in more passionate and effective ministry to others.

I would like to make you a promise. If you read this book all the way through, you'll notice a difference in your Bible reading. You will experi-ence a fresh excitement for God's Word, and you will see things you've never seen before in the Scriptures. Even if you don't apply *all* of the tools, you will still find yourself coming alive to the Bible. I'm convinced that you will be amazed at the beauty, depth, richness, and thrill of the Bible, though you may have been reading it for years.

GET RID OF BOREDOM

If the Bible is full of inspiring truth, spiritual revelation, penetrating insights, and even splashes of humor, why do many Christians complain that Bible reading is boring? Why do many believers skip it altogether or read only short passages before falling asleep at night?

We become bored when we get stuck for a long time in one place or when we're engaged in a repetitive activity. Long exposure to an environ-ment where the setting is dreary (think doctor's office) and monotonous activities deprive our brains of the stimulation they need to stay engaged. As a result, boredom sets in.

This happens with Bible study. Imagine opening your Bible (yawn). You look at the same scenery once again, read the same stories and records of ancient history you've read dozens of times before, and you see them the same way you've always seen them. The problem is repetition: We read the same words and draw from them the same meaning and emphasis every time. Our familiar, assumed interpretations obscure any new insights that God might want to unveil. We assume we already know what a passage means, so when we read it again it sounds like the same old stuff.

I know firsthand how easy it is to become overfamiliar with a fixed interpretation of Scripture. My dad is a first-class Bible teacher. From infancy I heard him teaching the Bible every Sunday morning and every Sunday and Wednesday evening. (I probably began to actually listen to him when I was in junior high school.) For the longest time when I read the Bible, I never bothered to ask, "What do these words mean?" because I thought I already knew.

When I first began teaching the Bible to other people, I pretty much taught what I had heard my dad teach. If I had a problem understanding a challenging passage, I would revert to my father's exposition. Though I still have great respect for Dad's teaching, I know that if I am going to truly study the Bible, *I* have to study the Bible. Listening to someone else teach is not the same as hearing God for myself. When I come to the Scriptures, I want to hear God's voice, find a profound revelation, and uncover a meaning to the Scripture that has specific application to my life and circumstances.

Our understanding of the Bible is formed more than we know by Bible teachers who have impressed us with their profound knowledge or have intimidated us with their authoritarian style. It's easy to assume that we don't need to hear the Bible's message for ourselves because someone has already told us all we need to know. But the result is a secondhand knowledge. When we read the Bible, the thoughts that spring into our mind are not always inspired by the Holy Spirit's speaking through the text; they are simply the lessons inherited from our favorite Bible teachers. When we study the Scriptures, we ought to be looking for something we missed in prior readings, something that was hidden from us but now is coming to light.

If we refuse to push ourselves to new understandings, we fail to hear a fresh and specific message from God. If we assume there is only one way to interpret a passage, then our real focus is on a human's interpretation rather than the biblical text itself. Sometimes listening to God in the Scripture means calling into question an earlier interpretation and looking for one that goes deeper. Otherwise we fall victim to rationalism, a problem that controlled biblical thinking for more than two centuries.

BREAK THE LEGACY OF RATIONALISM

During the nineteenth century, Christianity was seriously challenged by the intellectual assault of rationalism and the scientific method. The veracity of the biblical record was being questioned, and believers sought new ways to defend the faith. Conservative theologians devised scientific methods of biblical interpretation. In fact, Bible scholar Bernard Ramm defined hermeneutics as the "science of the correct interpretation of the Bible."[1] Thus Christians adopted the scientific bias for precision and technology, and these interpretive tools were passed on to us.[2]

Eventually two schools of interpretation emerged: liberal and conservative. Both schools were looking for the true meaning of the Scriptures. The liberal school treated the Bible as a human composition. Its scholars developed the discipline of higher criticism to nail down such questions as a book's authorship, its date of composition, and its cultural and historical background. Liberal scholars felt free to rearrange texts and books of the Bible to address what they saw as errors made by ancient scribes, while rejecting or reshaping anything that was implausible or offensive to the modern mind.

Conservative scholars, meanwhile, searched for God's revealed truth contained in the text. They were also concerned with the issues of higher criticism, but they had greater confidence in church tradition regarding authorship and the accepted sequence of biblical texts. Both schools believed their methods were scientific, rational, and effective.

THE BIG IDEA:

"Scientific" methods of biblical interpretation, both liberal and conservative, grew out of the rationalism of the modern era. The beliefs and perspectives of modernism, however, no longer reflect the dominant concerns of our culture.

These "scientific" methods of biblical interpretation, both liberal and conservative, did not always serve to bring out the deeper meanings contained in Scripture. And while the scientific method addresses the concerns of rationalism, it fails to address the questions and dominant concerns of today's culture. Biblical scholars are now discovering the value of new interpretive methods. For instance, interpreters are wondering what we have lost in overlooking the work of the early church fathers. One work, *The Ancient Christian Commentary on Scripture,*[3] has been embraced by Orthodox Christians and Roman Catholics as well as evangelical Christians. This is just one example of how new (and in some cases, ancient) tools and approaches are being used to open our eyes to deeper truth.

THE ONE RIGHT ANSWER

Conservative biblical scholarship, in response to the skepticism of rationalism, formulated the guiding principle that there is one correct interpretation for every biblical passage. The result was that believers came to think the same thoughts, draw the same conclusions, and make the same applications from a passage every time they read it. Some of those applications effectively addressed life two hundred years ago but have little or nothing to say to us today.

The assumption that each passage has only one correct interpretation is both helpful and harmful. It is helpful, because some things in the Bible are "hard to understand, which ignorant and unstable people distort" (2 Peter 3:16). If there were no standards, then anyone could build any theological framework he wanted. Not all interpretations are equally valid or helpful. As a result, we need a method that will help us evaluate interpretations and exclude those that are useless or even harmful.

I sat one time in a church where the preacher read a passage from Matthew 26 that included the phrase, "[Jesus] went a little farther, and fell on his face, and prayed" (Matthew 26:39, KJV). The preacher then expanded on the idea that we all need to go "a little farther" in our Christian experience. We not only needed to do this in our prayer lives and our Bible reading, but—the sermon was building to its climax—we needed to go a little further in our financial contributions. It was clear that this pastor was mangling the text to manipulate his audience. Knowing the "correct meaning" of a text will help us discern such bogus interpretations.

On the other hand, the one-correct-interpretation assumption can be limiting and even harmful because it assumes that once we know the true meaning of a passage, we no longer need to look for other levels of meaning. Some Christians may be afraid to look for other meanings, thinking they might fall into false doctrine. However, there are safeguards that enable us to avoid this danger. The unfortunate consequence of closing off other possible meanings is that reading the same passage in the same way keeps us from going deeper into the Scriptures. This is one reason people leave the Bible lying on the nightstand and turn on the television instead.

ONE TRUTH, MULTIPLE MEANINGS

Take a look at the number of times Jesus asked His audience, "Haven't you read…?" In many cases He quoted Old Testament passages that they already knew very well. Of course they had read the Genesis account of Adam and Eve, but they had failed to see what Jesus pointed out (see Matthew 19:3-12). Jesus' interpretation of Scripture was never bound by the tradition and teaching of the rabbinical schools of His time. He explored the text to find meanings no one had ever seen, though they had read the same words He was explaining.

Of course, one might argue that since Jesus is God, He had authority to interpret Scripture apart from the systems current in His day. Then I suppose we would have to argue that Peter and Paul also were able to reinterpret Scripture because they were apostles. But then there were the church fathers who used both Greek and Hebrew methods of interpretation as well as following the example of Peter and Paul (who reviewed Old Testament Scriptures in search of references to Jesus Christ). John Calvin's interpretation of Scripture was innovative in its time. In fact, the history of interpretation reveals an ongoing process of innovation and improvement. To halt that process in our time and claim we have arrived at the *only* true reading of the Bible is the height of egoism and sinful pride.

The Bible itself teaches us that while there may be one clear truth in a text, that truth is open to multiple meanings. This is not to say that *any* meaning is possible or that all interpretations are equally valid—there are rules that define and govern correct interpretations. But examine a text like Jeremiah 31:15, "This is what the LORD says: 'A voice is heard in Ramah, mourning and great weeping, Rachel weeping for her children and refusing to be comforted, because her children are no more.'"

Careful analysis tells us that this verse refers to the children of Judah who had been taken into captivity by the Babylonians. The passage in Jeremiah goes on to promise they would one day return to Palestine; in fact, the people of Judah were to *stop grieving*. God meant to encourage them, because their "work will be rewarded" and "there is hope for your future" (Jeremiah 31:16-17). But Matthew, when he was writing his gospel, found *another* significant meaning for this text that probably never occurred to Jeremiah. In the light of Herod's attempt to kill the infant

Jesus, "Rachel weeping for her children" could be interpreted to describe the grief Bethlehem experienced over the murder of its babies (see Matthew 2:16-18). Thus the passage in Jeremiah is capable of yielding at least two different meanings, as shown in Scripture.

Still, you might wonder why, since we have access to sound Bible commentaries, we would want to attempt interpreting the Bible for ourselves. Here's a quick answer: First, if the Holy Spirit has planted multiple meanings in Scripture, we need to look for them. Second, the propositions that critical interpretations yield are often abstract—true to the text but disconnected from the practical concerns of daily living. Third, the purpose of reading the Bible is not only to learn its truth, but also—and at times, especially—to hear God speak to us in a very personal way.

A few weeks ago I was rereading Matthew 22 when something caught my eye. Jesus was presenting evidence for life after death to the Sadducees, and said to them, "But about the resurrection of the dead—have you not read what God said to you, 'I am the God of Abraham, the God of Isaac, and the God of Jacob'?" (22:31-32). Of course these experts in the law had read the passage He cited, so what are we missing in His question? Jesus said, "Have you not read *what God said to you,*" which is a revealing statement. God "spoke" to the Sadducees through the Scripture. Unfortunately, they failed to hear what God said. The Sadducees prided themselves on their knowledge of the Law (the first five books of the Bible), but in all their study they had never heard God speak personally to them concerning life after death.

We are in danger of falling into the same trap. We can study and interpret the Bible in such a way that we learn its truths yet never hear God speak to us. Of course, we read the Bible to observe and meditate on the information we find, to study its theological propositions, and to do in-depth research into its history, culture, and language. But even though we may find the most precise meaning of a passage, that does not exhaust all possible meanings. God may intend to use another meaning of the same passage to speak to us in a new way.

Rules of Correct Interpretation

Before we explore new tools for interpreting Scripture, let's clarify the assumptions and beliefs that will guide our study.

1. We will fully embrace the authority and reliability of the Scriptures. What the Bible says is true, and we are bound by its commands. The Bible is a sacred text that was inspired by God. The Bible is the revelation of God.

2. Scientific methods of interpretation are still necessary for a proper understanding of Scripture. We cannot dispense with historical-grammatical exegesis or inductive Bible study methods. Those methods, however, do not exhaust *all* possible meanings within a text.

3. The Bible speaks to the whole context of our lives, and it is crucial that we constantly look for its application to political, social, ethical, and aesthetic issues as well as to those that are spiritual and intellectual.

4. Related to the previous assumption is the requirement that we must be "doers of the word, and not hearers only" (James 1:22, KJV). There is no value in careful biblical interpretation if we don't intend to respond with our whole heart, mind, soul, and body to what we discover in God's Word.

5. God wants to communicate with you. God speaks to His people through the Scriptures. We do not study the Bible with a detached objectivity. As we read and interpret the Bible, we are listening for God's voice with the ears of our heart.

6. There is a difference between the Bible and our interpretation of the Bible. The Bible is inspired, our interpretations are not—they are in many cases our best guess based on the available evidence. (What we experience when God's Spirit gives us insight into a text's meaning is referred to as "illumination.") Nevertheless, the message of the gospel is undoubtedly clear

enough that we can confidently proclaim God's way of salvation to others.

7. Every generation of Christians has the responsibility to discover what the Bible has to say to its specific time, place, and culture. The Bible is unchanging, but it yields interpretations and applications that speak to every new development in the human situation and every change in culture and society.

8. The Bible is a sacred document, and it will not yield its spiritual meaning to an unspiritual mind (see Matthew 11:25-26; 1 Corinthians 2:12-16). Common sense is helpful for Bible study, but it is an insufficient tool for discovering a text's full meaning. For this reason it's critical that we approach Bible study with much prayer before, during, and after.

9. If we approach the Bible with humility, we'll make much better progress than if we come with a skeptical, hostile, proud, or even "objective" mind. The Bible requires us to accept its impact on our lives. To learn its mysteries and meanings, we must humbly surrender to its authority and truth.

10. Whatever else our reading of the Bible may do for us, it must bring us closer to Jesus Christ, not only in relationship with Him and His church, but also in conformity to the life He lived and taught. We are a people of the Book *and* the Person, because Jesus and His Word are so interrelated there is no way to separate them. Without the Bible, we have no Jesus, but to follow the arrow of Scripture is to arrive at Jesus.

If you're looking for useful tools to help you do a "close reading" of Scripture, please join me on this journey. I can promise you a great adventure as you hear God speak to you regarding His will and your own life's circumstances. Surrender to the transforming power of the Bible and you will come to know Jesus Christ better. You will become the kind of Christian who can make a real difference in this world, and your life will never again be the same.

CHAPTER 1

LAYERS OF MEANING

Paying Attention to What Lies Within the Biblical Text

Lord Christ from out his treasury
Brings forth things new and old:
We have those treasures in earthen vessels,
In parables he told,
And in the single images
Of seed, and fish, and stone,
Or, shaped in deed and miracle,
To living poems grown.

JAMES MCAULEY

The above lines are taken from James McAuley's *An Art of Poetry*.[1] Did you skip over the poem, assuming its message was irrelevant to this chapter? If you read the poem, did you think about its meaning? Because it is poetry, did you anticipate the rhyming word at the end of each stanza? Did you read it out loud so you could feel the rhythm of the verse? Perhaps you read these lines without consciously thinking about any of these things.

Try this exercise: Reread the poem, and concentrate on what goes on in your mind. Focus your attention on what you are thinking as you read. It will help if you describe aloud what you are doing. For example, "I'm thinking about Jesus Christ and His treasury. What is His 'treasury'? I'll read further down... Oh, His treasury is His parables, His teaching. Okay, now I'm wondering why the poet used the word *treasury?* Maybe this is a very old poem because I don't think most writers today would use that word."

WHAT TO THINK ABOUT

What happens when we read? Basically, our eyes take in a series of letters. As we read, we attempt to make sense of these written symbols and discover the message encoded in them. But we all know that reading is much more than decoding symbols.

Every sentence has a structure that is influenced by grammar, punctuation, and a number of other rules. There is also the writer's particular style. The sentences may be written in such a way that you discern a cadence to them. One of the benefits of being raised on the *King James Version* of the Bible is an appreciation for the music of a well-composed sentence. But there is still more to reading than the structure of sentences.

We read with a specific purpose in mind: to be entertained, inspired, informed, or comforted. We read for pleasure, to find help in solving a problem, or to advance our career. We read personal letters and e-mail to keep in touch with friends. We even read to kill time while waiting to board a flight or when picking up our kids at soccer practice. But there is still much more to reading.

Reading is the search for a meaning. To find the meaning, we piece together the thoughts in the text and look for a central idea. If the text didn't mean something to us, we wouldn't waste our time with it. But that brings us to a significant question: What determines the meaning? Is it determined by the author or by the historical circumstances that shaped the message? Does the meaning come from the words of the text, or do we create meaning as we read?

Since our goal is to find ways to discover the meaning in Scripture, let's apply these questions to the Bible. Is the meaning of a biblical text in the mind of God, who inspired Scripture's various writers, or is it found in the writers' historical situation and culture or in the circumstances of the original readers (for example, the challenge of living in Corinth for the readers of Paul's Corinthian letters)? Or are we to conclude that the actual meaning is contained in the words of the text, independent of all other factors? Of course, when we are reading Scripture, we also must ask: Does the true meaning come to us only when the Holy Spirit illumines our minds to understand the text?

These questions have given rise to intense scholarly debate. Some interpreters look for meaning in the structure of the text, while others try to get inside the mind of the writer, and still others examine the readers' response to the text. It's valuable to grapple with these questions, because it leads us to some fascinating new ways of looking at the Bible.

THE BIG IDEA:

Reading is *always* an exercise in interpretation, which is the search for meaning. Recent studies in interpretive methods (hermeneutics and literary theory) can enhance our understanding of the Bible.

HOW TO FIND MEANING

No matter what we read, we discover meaning through interpretation. Much of the time, we're unaware of the ways we apply interpretative techniques. But if we are reading a technical manual that is over our head or a poem that is a bit obscure, we realize we can't interpret the message with only one reading. Then we become more conscious of the work that is required to interpret the text.

With every experience of daily life, we are making interpretations. Even a message as simple as the word *stop* on a traffic sign can be interpreted in a variety of ways. Some people interpret it to mean, "Bring the car to a complete halt behind the white line before proceeding through the intersection." For other motorists the sign means, "Slow down a little before rolling into the intersection." Still others find a different meaning depending on circumstances: "Stop sometimes, but not if you're in a hurry." For Californians who are making a right turn, the stop sign holds no meaning whatsoever. To them it says, "Don't even bother."

Occasionally you'll meet Christians who insist they do not interpret the Bible but take it at face value. What they are implying (I think) is that they are getting God's ideas straight from God without any human interference. But it's impossible to read without interpreting, even if we're unaware of the process. And as we read, few of us realize how much our chosen interpretive method controls our understanding of what we're reading.

WAYS OF INTERPRETING

Some interpretive methods are excellent tools for finding authentic and useful meanings, others are only mediocre, and still others are actually dangerous. One particularly unhelpful method is to read a passage and immediately jump to an application. A person might read a verse such as John 1:1: "In the beginning was the Word, and the Word was with God, and the Word was God," then say, "What God is telling us is to read our Bibles because the Word is God." That sort of reflexive interpretation actually prevents people from discovering the text's meaning. A better approach is to begin with the question "What does this text *say* and what does it *mean?*" From the meaning we will discover the significance of the text and, in turn, what God is saying to us through that text. An even more challenging and fruitful approach is to ask, "What question does this text answer?" (Try it!)

Another shortcoming is to interpret the Bible through the particular bias of a certain religious culture or theological system. People who share a similar background and have all been trained in the same method of interpretation may believe that they alone have discovered the one, true meaning of Scripture. Some Christians will claim that those who disagree with their interpretation don't have the Holy Spirit or the proper framework for interpreting prophecy, as just one example. Or they might insist that we can't understand the Bible without the guidance of a particular scholar, such as Thomas Aquinas or John Calvin.

These are the sorts of mistakes we want to avoid. By thinking about how we read and interpret the Bible, we can become aware of the strengths and weaknesses of our own method of interpretation and discover the value of what other people have to say. It's essential that we learn a variety of methods that will help us find deeper meanings.

Communication, in its most streamlined form, consists of three parts: the sender, the receiver, and the message (or author, reader, and text). Similarly, interpretation, when streamlined, looks for meaning in either the sender, the receiver, the message, or some combination of the three. But to find the meaning we'll need a variety of tools. One particular method may lead to a dead end or to an irrelevant meaning, while another may reveal a previously undiscovered vein of gold.

THE DANGERS OF INTERPRETATION

While scholarly research into forms of literature and theories of interpretation can yield great rewards, they also bring inherent dangers when applied to reading the Bible. Even some of the helpful interpretive methods grow out of philosophies that are incompatible with Christian faith. Some of those philosophies deny absolute truth, literal meaning, or that the intention of an author has anything to do with the meaning of the text. If we were to embrace the *entire* philosophy that lies behind some interpretive methods, we would deny important teachings in the Bible.

For this reason, it's crucial that we apply wisdom and spiritual discernment (see Philippians 1:9-11; 1 Thessalonians 5:21-22). We also need to apply certain safeguards. For example, we will never discard or abandon the literal sense of a text. Careful analysis of the literal meaning of a passage always comes before any subsequent meaning. If we land on a meaning that contradicts the text's literal meaning or the literal meaning of any other biblical passage, then the new meaning must be reexamined. The easiest way to track the literal meaning of a passage is to make use of the best available Bible commentaries, drawing from a variety of orthodox views.

When we use the term *literal meaning*, we keep in mind that some words or phrases are idioms, analogies, metaphors, or hyperboles (a literary form of exaggeration). For example, the phrase "a son of..." or "children of..." in the Old Testament is used literally in some places but as a figure of speech in other places.[2] When Jesus spoke of "living water," He was not referring to a liquid substance. Hence, the literal meaning of a text refers to the way a passage would be understood in normal discourse without looking for elaborate allegories to lend a "spiritual meaning" to every word.

A second essential safeguard is the study of historical context, biblical context, grammar, and Christian theology. Any meaning that conflicts with Christian doctrine or the reasoned study of a passage must be carefully reexamined. While benefiting from the use of new interpretive tools, we are still tethered to the Reformers' historical-grammatical method of interpretation. This means that we do our best to follow the grammatical rules of the language we are studying—including its unique use of words and phrases—and we do our best to understand the whole sweep of history in which Scripture was written, including geography and climate, religious rites and practices of neighboring nations, and the cultural norms and customs of biblical settings.

A third safeguard is to remember that when we interpret the Bible, we are looking for God's divine revelation: What does God have to say about Himself, humankind, His relation to the world and its people, sin, salvation, and so on? Any interpretation that reduces the Bible to human thoughts, experiences, or ideas must be avoided. Without a proper respect for the Bible as God's Word, we're not in a position to hear God speak to us.

There are some who argue that since the Bible is a unique book, no method of interpretation should be used other than the historical-grammatical method. This argument is weak because the historical-grammatical method itself is not holy—there isn't one divinely sanctioned method of biblical interpretation. Neither is there any method that can be applied exclusively to the Bible and not to secular literature. We must bear in mind that God determined to deliver His truth to us as a written document. Though the message is divine, the form of its presentation is literature. Therefore the rules that apply to all literature apply also to the Bible.

To better understand this point, let's consider the "other Word of God," that is, Jesus Christ (see John 1:1). According to John 1:14, "The Word became flesh and made his dwelling among us." Theologically we refer to this movement of God into human flesh as the Incarnation. Jesus came in the form of a man and was subjected to every temptation and condition that we all suffer. In a similar way, the Bible that comes to us as literature is subject to methods of interpretation common to all literature, although the truth it reveals is uniquely divine. The difference between the Bible and other forms of literature is that with the Bible we need a variety of interpretive methods *plus* the Holy Spirit. This leads to the next point.

A fourth necessary safeguard is to remember that our ultimate goal is to hear what the Holy Spirit is saying to us. As we study, we are asking God's Spirit to personally direct our reading and interpretation. Therefore, any particular method is merely a tool we use to help achieve our ultimate goal. What is different about our approach to interpretation is the recognition that the Bible is an inspired document and we are always dependent on the Holy Spirit for a true understanding of it.

There is something providential about what we find when we apply a method of interpretation to Scripture. What catches our eye, what hooks our thoughts, what creates confusion are all spontaneous and immediate experiences directed by God's Spirit. If biblical interpretation is an art as well as a science, it is also a spiritual and Spirit-led endeavor.

LITERAL AND FIGURATIVE MEANINGS

Prior to the rise of rationalism and its emphasis on the "science of interpretation," one of the popular methods of interpretation was allegory—a method that transformed people, places, and objects of the Bible into symbols that represented spiritual truths and realities. For example, a horse, sword, or palm branch could be loaded with complex and spiritual meanings. Old Testament events could be read as dramas that reveal the person of Jesus Christ. Rather than helping to clarify a meaning, however, allegorical interpretation often was whimsical, revealing the ingenuity of the interpreter rather than the intended meaning of the text.

One huge benefit of new interpretive methods is they provide us with a healthy option to the risky use of allegory, which almost always entails overinterpretation.[3] An allegory is not the same thing as a biblical "type" (for example, the sacrifices of the Old Testament are a "type" of Jesus' sacrifice on the cross), although typology can also be taken too far.

Shortly after the time of Christ, many of the church fathers, including careful theologians such as Augustine, employed the allegorical method. Allegorical interpretation did not disappear in the modern age but has heavily influenced devotional literature even among evangelicals from the 1940s to the present. Some of the most destructive yet widespread heresies of recent history have been based on allegory.

The methods of interpretation that we will use are not allegorical. Rather, they involve taking the text at face value, then looking within, around, under, and through the text for other possible meanings. If we need to use our imaginations, it will not be to invent meanings but to help us wrap our minds around what is already there. Nevertheless, allegory has its uses and should not be totally shunned.

HOW WE GROW IN UNDERSTANDING

Not long ago at a conference for young Christian leaders, I was asked to field questions on a panel with other ministers. At one point I made the observation that popular culture has blurred the boundary between reality and fantasy, that today reality is considered to be a human invention rather than a stable fact. I suggested that we should be aware of the way people are inventing their own realities.

Another minister, responding to my comment, forcefully stated that Christians have a handle on reality because our reality is the Bible. He emphasized that, for us, reality is defined by God's Word. In a way, he claimed the moral high ground by siding with the Bible against cultural definitions. Yet even as he spoke, there was something naive, almost innocent, about his perceptions.

We like to think that we come to the Bible with our minds a blank slate waiting for God to inscribe His truth on them. We assume we are objective and detached researchers, that no prior claims on our thinking affect what we read. But to be honest, interpretation begins before we even pick up the Bible. We already have ideas about the importance of reading Scripture, the reliability of its contents, and what sort of information we will find there. The idea that "the Bible defines reality for us" is not derived from the Bible but is a rational conclusion we've drawn before we have even opened the Bible. In truth, our own experience of life and the assumptions of our culture color our interpretations of Scripture.

When I was a boy, I thought the phrase in Proverbs 17:17, "a brother is born for adversity," meant that little brothers were born to create nothing but trouble for older brothers. Much later I learned that brothers are born to help each other through adversity. The actual meaning is just the opposite of what I first thought.

It's true that the Bible gives us a number of reality bites in broad strokes. We learn from Scripture that God created the universe, that humans have a propensity for sin, that Jesus Christ died on a cross for our sins and three days later He rose from the dead. But does the Bible explain what the spirit-substance is that God is made of and how it differs from our material bodies? There are a host of questions for which the Bible offers no answers at all.

Some Christian communities teach that believers need an experience of God's Holy Spirit subsequent to salvation that they refer to as the "baptism of the Holy Spirit." They also teach that the proof someone has been "baptized in the Spirit" is the phenomenon of speaking in tongues. This is biblical "reality" for them, and they have an experience that validates what they believe. Does their reading of the Bible define reality for every Christian? Hardly. Millions of non-Pentecostal Christians have found a very different reality in the words of Scripture.

There are other important questions as well. Does the Bible explain the structure of an atom or tell us what the cold water of a mountain stream feels like on our bare feet? Does the Bible explain how a democracy operates or how constitutional government is formed? Hidden beneath the pious pretense that the Bible defines reality for us is the unhappy secret that the "reality" we North Americans claim to find in Scripture is identical to the reality of our Western worldview. In fact, our culture—not the Scriptures—forms our view of reality. It is more accurate to say the Bible can *redefine* our reality through a long and painstaking process of study and practice. But few people have honestly ventured into that frightening and destabilizing process.

Think about the process of growth we see in the words of Paul: "When I was a child, I talked like a child, I thought like a child, I reasoned like a child. When I became a man, I put childish ways behind me" (1 Corinthians 13:11). Hopefully, we all can say that our understanding of Scripture today is more mature than it was twenty years ago. Likewise, our understanding today is childish compared to what we hope it will be twenty years from now.

I imagine you've had the experience of revisiting a place you haven't seen since childhood. Perhaps it's your old elementary school, a church you attended as a child, or the house where a grandparent once lived. There is a common reaction we have when returning to such a place: "I remember this as being so much *bigger* than it is." When we look at our world or read the Bible, we assume we are *directly perceiving reality* without any intermediate influence. Our view of tangibles (objects, people, and places) and intangibles (truth, spirit, salvation, and so on) is affected by a complex matrix of physical, cultural, and personal factors. We all look at the world through a number of lenses. When we encounter our own conflicting perceptions of reality, it's legitimate to ask: "What changed, the size of Grandma's house, or my perception of the house?"

Some would argue that the Bible's intent is not to define reality but to reveal important truths such as God's attributes and nature, the believer's true identity, the way of atonement, and so on. On the other hand, the Holy Spirit works in our lives to define, explain, teach, and apply the truth of the Bible to our hearts through His work of illumination (see John 14:26; 16:12-15). Of course we want the Bible to shape our reality, but we have to admit that our reality also shapes our interpretation of the Bible. God intends for us to read and understand the Bible within our own context. But we can also learn to be sensitive to the context of other people and listen carefully to *their* interpretation. Our Western worldview is very different from two-thirds of the world's population— even those who are Christians and who study the Bible just as we do. Can we humble ourselves as Paul humbled himself and say, "Now we see but a poor reflection as in a mirror" (1 Corinthians 13:12)?

The Bible does have a significant message for us about reality. The Scriptures serve us by destabilizing our reality so that we can learn to put our faith in God, not in our culture (see 2 Corinthians 1:9; Hebrews 12:26-27). The Bible raises questions about the unspoken assumptions of our culture, its values and its exploitation of sinful desire, its dogmatism and its conspicuous consumption. If we are going to seriously study the Bible, we must submit our reality to its scrutiny and interrogation. We must be prepared to confess that we have been wrong about some things and we need to repent. We do not come to the Bible only to drill it with questions—who, what, where, when, why, how—but we come *to be questioned* by the sacred text. For the Bible to define reality for us, we must first confess that our view of reality needs to be redeemed and redefined.

With humility and complete openness to God, let's explore new methods of interpretation that promise to bring us closer to what God has to say to us today. Let's begin a life-changing journey in the Scriptures, trusting in God's Spirit to give us eyes to see and ears to hear.

CHAPTER 2

IS IT AN APPLE
OR AN ORANGE?

Paying Attention to Classes
of Biblical Literature

Last year I attended a four-day conference in Texas. When I returned home, my wife, Barbara, greeted me with a hug, told me she missed me, then filled me in on everything that had happened while I was gone. Later that evening when I checked my e-mail, there was a message from Barbara —something she had sent the day before. I won't share the particulars but will simply say that the warmth of her affectionate words touched my heart.

For some reason, the process of writing out her feelings allowed my wife to say more than she could when speaking to me, and she was able to communicate in a different style. Reading her message in the quiet of my study enabled me to concentrate more on what she had to say than if we tried to engage in conversation amid the usual din that fills our home. Oral communication is sometimes at a disadvantage when conveying certain kinds of messages. This is especially true when we want to communicate difficult or intimate aspects of a relationship.

There are passages of Scripture that address fractured relationships or seek to mend a schism between people or within a community. Take a moment to compare these two passages:

How good and pleasant it is
   when brothers live together in unity!
It is like the precious oil poured on the head,
   running down on the beard,
running down on Aaron's beard,
   down upon the collar of his robes.
It is as if the dew of Hermon
   were falling on Mount Zion.
For there the LORD bestows his blessing,
   even life forevermore. (Psalm 133)

I appeal to you, brothers, in the name of our Lord Jesus Christ, that all of you agree with one another so that there may be no divisions among you and that you may be perfectly united in mind and thought. (1 Corinthians 1:10)

Both passages address the same subject: unity among brothers. However, apart from sharing the same theme, these quotations could hardly be more different. The psalm is poetic and makes use of descriptive expressions and metaphors, whereas Paul's appeal in 1 Corinthians is clear and unadorned in its directness. The passages differ in style even though they share the same theme, because David composed a poem and Paul wrote a letter; they are two different types of literature.

I'm sure you've heard the expression, "It's like comparing apples to oranges." In other words, some things are so dissimilar it is unfair to make comparisons between them. Are you hungry for something that is tangy and full of juice and vitamin C? Eat an orange. Do you prefer something sweet and crunchy? Try an apple. Although they both belong to the category of fruit, they are different enough that each can be appreciated for its own qualities and not how it compares to the other.

The same is true with various types of literature. Poetry is different from narrative, short story is different from novel, fiction is different from nonfiction, and within the fiction category, romance is different from sci-fi. One way to talk about the differences in literature is to use the word *genre*, a term borrowed from the French language, which in turn borrowed it from Latin *(genus)*. In science, genus is a classification of items that share the same general characteristics. A genre is a type within a system of classification relating to art and literary criticism.

Common sense and everyday experience tell us that it's useful to recognize different categories of literature. Browsing a bookstore or library would be incredibly confusing if someone had not arranged the books according to their types: psychology, autobiography, history, fiction, and classics, to name a few. If the same book is found in more than one section of a bookstore, it fits more than one category due to sharing characteristics in common with those other categories. A Christian book on improving relationships might be found both in the religion section and in the self-help section. However, there is no book that will be found in *every* section.

Likewise, various parts of the Bible fall into different classes of literature. No type of biblical literature is superior to another, but a particular genre tends to be better suited to accomplishing certain goals. And when we think about genres of literature in the Bible, we need to acknowledge that there is a lot of overlap and interweaving of different literary forms in the text.

THE BIG IDEA:

There are different classes (genres) of literature, and each has its own characteristics. Knowing what type of literature you are reading gives you clues to the meaning of the text—even before you read the first page!

If the suggestion that we identify the literary forms in Scripture makes you uncomfortable, consider the following. Our Bible consists of two main divisions, the Old and New Testaments. The Gospels in the New

Testament have a unique style that differs considerably from New Testament letters. The Old Testament, according to the words of Jesus, is made up of the Law, the Prophets, and the Psalms (see Luke 24:44). To look at the Scriptures in terms of different genres comes naturally to most Bible students, including, it seems, Jesus Himself.

THE VALUE OF BIBLICAL GENRES

One way to think of different types of literature is to imagine an author and a reader agreeing to certain rules that will govern how they will discuss a particular topic. The author is likely to know what genre she is going to use before she begins writing. In general, the reader also knows the genre before he begins reading. If I pick up a science textbook, I don't expect it to be entertaining. If I were writing a poem, I wouldn't expect people to read it to learn how to repair a computer. So the genre is a starting point for both author and reader, more or less laying out the rules of the game.

A tremendous benefit of understanding literary genres is that it gives us a clearer picture of the intent, mood, and "sound" of the author's voice. For a couple of years, my younger sister lived in London, and we began a short-lived e-mail correspondence. Cheryl and I gave up, though, when we realized our attempts at keeping in touch electronically had failed dismally. Our frustration had to do with the elements of communication that don't come across well in an e-mail message. Here is how my sister explained it: "When you have a face-to-face conversation, a lot is communicated nonverbally—the upturned corner of the mouth in a slight smile, a wink, a nudge, and a hundred other ways that we speak with body language. But writing lacks intonation, volume, and pitch. You cannot know if the other person is yelling or crying."

It's unfortunate that we can't hear God's tone of voice when reading some of His statements. We may interpret His words as if they were shouted in anger when they actually were spoken with a sob. We can't hear the inflection in Jesus' voice when He called the Pharisees hypocrites and whitewashed tombs (see Matthew 23:27). Was He sarcastic, was He spitting out His words in frustration, was He matter-of-fact, or was there pain in His voice?

Fortunately, we have clues to help us identify the writer's tone of voice. By paying attention to the type of literature we are reading, we have a head start on knowing how the author wants us to interpret his writing. Different literary genres reflect different modes of expression. This helps us determine if the author is shouting, whispering, weeping, rejoicing, or simply giving a straightforward report. Genre also gives readers an idea of what the whole text is about when we begin to read the first sentence. We can't predict what the author will say, but knowing the genre of the book or passage gives us a general idea of its parameters. We catch the essence of the whole text because we know something about the genre being used.

As readers, we bring different sets of expectations to different genres. We don't have the same expectations while reading science fiction that we have when reading a newspaper. We even have different expectations reading front-page headlines than we do the sports page. If the text is a poem, we look for features like meter, rhyme, and metaphors. If the text is a murder mystery, we look for clues as to who might be the killer.

When we pick up the Bible, we know that a psalm reads differently from a description of Jewish ceremonial law in Leviticus. A letter written by Paul bears little similarity to the apocalyptic prophecy of Revelation. Genre gives us a huge clue as to how the author intended us to interpret the text.

THE WHOLE VS. ITS PARTS

Suppose you come home from work and you're in the mood to read something. You grab a magazine and thumb through its pages. Before you start reading, you wonder, *What is this article about?* To satisfy your curiosity, you read the title, then the first paragraph of the article. Or you scan a few pages to find subject headings and to check for photos, diagrams, or charts. These are common features of a person's reading habits, but isn't it a little strange that we want to know what a story is about *before* we read it?

We look for clues to a book's meaning before we start reading because it helps us interpret the book once we turn to page one. The title of the book might give us an idea of what to expect, or perhaps it will simply arouse our interest as it raises more questions. The same can be said for chapter titles. As we read, we are constantly circling around from the whole of the book to its component parts and then back to the whole. The message of the entire book is dependent on the individual words, and the words take on special meaning only when joined together to communicate a book's message.

Think of a circle, which at first glance appears to be a solid geometric shape. The circle is, in fact, made up of a series of small dots so close together that they touch. The circle is the sum of all the dots, and each dot is one unit of the circle. In other words, the individual dots form the circle, but the circle itself defines the *role* of each dot. In literature, the text is like the circle, and the words are like the dots. This is what literary scholars call the *hermeneutical circle,* going from the whole message to the individual parts, then back to the whole again.

When we begin reading, we can't predict what words, sentences, or ideas will follow—we must wait until we come to them. As we read each word we look for its relationship to what we have already read. We are moving from the big picture of the whole text to the smaller units within the text and back again. We circle around the text because we're constantly testing our understanding of the whole to the parts and the parts to the whole.

This is a crucial process for Bible study. For example, when we read the book of Romans, we want to discover Paul's message to the Christians in Rome. Then we want to see how he develops that message and the truths he explains and the points he emphasizes. However, when we first begin to read Romans, we have to make an educated guess at his message.

The further we read, the better we will know if our guess was correct or if it must be modified and then modified again as we continue to read.

A fairly typical mistake of novice Bible students is to begin reading one of the Gospels, for instance, and immediately start doing word studies. Sometimes they will build a Bible study around one word or sentence. But the sentences must be understood in the context of the whole. Therefore we have to keep swinging our attention from the general message of the book to the specific thought in the sentence to make certain the two are related.

If we know something about biblical genre, then we have a considerable advantage in predicting the message. We still need to give the book a thorough reading, but simply having a general idea of its place in Scripture and the kind of information we can expect to find in it will help form our initial idea of its purpose.

BASIC GENRES IN THE BIBLE

I want to keep this part really simple, because people can get carried away and find hundreds of genres and even subgenres in the Bible. For example, the psalms are a subclass of the Wisdom Literature, but the book of Psalms can also be broken into psalms of praise and psalms of lament. The psalms of praise can be further divided into praise of the community and praise of the individual.[1] And that is only the beginning.

We will keep our list of literary genres rather basic. They include:

History. The history of the Bible is usually more than a record of events; it is history that teaches lessons or shows how events lead to a specific outcome. Much of the Bible's history is storytelling, and some is recorded statistics or lists, such as genealogies, items donated to the upkeep of the tabernacle, or stations and duties of the priests.

Wisdom. The books from Job to the Song of Songs make up the Wisdom Literature, but you will also come across a sprinkling of this genre embedded within many other books. The wisdom genre consists mostly of poetry, proverbs, sage discourses, and songs. Scholars also look closely at the *structure* of wisdom writing, which frequently makes use of chiasmus and parallelism, two devices that are examined later in this chapter.

Prophetic books. These writings include prophecies that predict future events, including the apocalyptic literature found in Daniel and Revelation. But the majority of biblical prophecy consists of commands and warnings that addressed specific historical situations.

Law. There are many long passages in Scripture that list, explain, and elaborate on God's commandments.

Teaching and sermons. There isn't a book of sermons in the Bible—although some commentators believe Deuteronomy consists of five sermons that Moses delivered to the people of Israel. The Bible's sermons appear in many different places. For example, the book of Acts includes a number of sermons, including Peter's Pentecost message (see Acts 2:14-40), Stephen's defense before the Sanhedrin (see Acts 7), and several of Paul's sermons and speeches.

Letters. A large percentage of the New Testament was written originally in the form of personal letters intended to encourage believers, settle disputes, and provide more information about Jesus Christ and the Christian faith.

GENRE QUESTIONS

There are particular questions we can ask to help us use the genre of a book or passage to help target its meaning.

- Is this text from the Old Testament or the New Testament?
- What is the genre of this book in general and this passage in particular?
- What are the characteristics of this genre? (See the preceding section.)

- Why would the author choose this genre for communicating his message?
- What is it about the message that makes this genre appropriate?
- What knowledge do the author and reader share about this genre?
- What expectations does the reader have about this genre?
- What does this genre *do?* Does it tell a story, argue a point, issue a command, evoke an emotion, clarify an event or belief, teach a lesson, or provide insights into how or why a situation occurred?

Besides the questions we ask of the text, genre also suggests that there are questions the text asks of us. Are we being asked to feel, understand, or take action? The text has an intended effect on the reader. For example:

- Is the intended effect of this genre instructive, emotive, directive, or something else? If we read a passage from the book of Romans, we expect to learn something, but if we are reading a psalm we may expect to *feel* something. The teaching of Jesus often demands that we *do* something.
- Does this genre ask me to be sharp and astute or to relax and enjoy the read? Sometimes our power of observation is more acute when we are imagining the story rather than intensely analyzing every word. Our imaginations often help us to see more of what is in the text.
- Does God speak directly through this genre (for example, prophecy) or indirectly (parable)?
- What skills and additional work might this genre require of me? Some genres require a bit of historical or linguistic research. Others require detective-like skills for finding all the hidden clues.

How to Use This New Tool

With the ability to identify the literary genres in the Bible, we have a valuable interpretive tool at our disposal. As we begin to use this tool, our first step is to draw a line (figuratively speaking) around the passage we want to study. Where does the passage begin and end? The passage will contain one continuous unit of thought, so when the thought shifts, you have moved to a new passage. To simplify the process I have chosen a passage from Isaiah 5:

I will sing for the one I love
    a song about his vineyard:
My loved one had a vineyard
    on a fertile hillside.
He dug it up and cleared it of stones
    and planted it with the choicest vines.
He built a watchtower in it
    and cut out a winepress as well.
Then he looked for a crop of good grapes,
    but it yielded only bad fruit.
"Now you dwellers in Jerusalem and men of Judah,
    judge between me and my vineyard.
What more could have been done for my vineyard
    than I have done for it?
When I looked for good grapes,
    why did it yield only bad?
Now I will tell you
    what I am going to do to my vineyard:
I will take away its hedge,
    and it will be destroyed;
I will break down its wall,
    and it will be trampled.
I will make it a wasteland,
    neither pruned nor cultivated,
    and briars and thorns will grow there.

I will command the clouds
   not to rain on it."

The vineyard of the LORD Almighty
   is the house of Israel,
and the men of Judah
   are the garden of his delight.
And he looked for justice, but saw bloodshed;
   for righteousness, but heard cries of distress. (Isaiah 5:1-7)

IDENTIFYING THE GENRE

Before we even began reading, we knew that the book of Isaiah belongs to the prophetic genre. So from the start we could have been asking ourselves, What is it that God is saying through His prophet? Who is addressed in this prophecy, and what were the circumstances that called for this message? All those questions can be answered fairly easily, but something unusual has already captured our attention. Did you realize that Isaiah *sang* this prophecy? He began, "I will sing for the one I love a song about his vineyard." Further, the structure of the Hebrew text, written in the form of a psalm, confirms that this is a song. We are reading the words of a song, and songs belong to a different genre than prophetic speech. So here is an instance of two genres converging. Prophetic speech can sometimes take the form of inspired, artistic expression.

There is still another observation we need to make about the genre of this passage, but first we should think about the message. The last verse clarifies the images that are used, so we know God is the "loved one" who owned the vineyard, and the people of Israel and Judah were the vineyard. God had been wronged by His people. He had given them every advantage to produce "good grapes." Instead, they produced "only bad fruit."

If we have a knowledge of Israel's history, we might assume the "good grapes" referred to Israel's loyalty to God, His covenant, and His law. The nation, however, kept slipping into idolatry and pagan practices. The northern empire, which had seen a rapid succession of kings rise and fall, was about to come to an end and its people carried off into captivity. Meanwhile, the kings of Judah (the southern kingdom) were unable to sustain a strong spiritual and moral commitment among their subjects.

This is worthwhile background, but in this passage Isaiah was concerned about Israel's and Judah's disloyalty to God in a more specific way, and the main concern was not idolatry. With the exception of King Ahaz, idolatry was not a problem for Judah's rulers during Isaiah's ministry. The prophet's song was meant to address injustice and violence (see verse 7). God had given commandments to His people that legislated, not only their relationship with Him, but also their relationship with one another. They were especially responsible for the weak, poor, and vulnerable members of their community. The message addresses a sociological problem, the "bad fruit" of injustice.

DECIPHERING THE SYMBOLS

We know that Isaiah is making use of the wisdom genre as well as the prophetic; therefore, we may anticipate his use of metaphors and symbols. The question of metaphor is how is the image that is used similar to the subject it represents—i.e., how is a vineyard like Israel? In verse 7 Isaiah spells out what the symbols mean. Once we know their meaning, what is the *message* of this song?

Israel and Judah had enjoyed God's favor and help for hundreds of years. He rescued them from Egypt, revealed to them His law, taught them how to approach Him in worship, "planted" them in the Promised Land, and spoke to them constantly through His prophets. If anyone should have prospered spiritually, these people should have. But instead of producing the results one would expect, the people ignored God's laws regarding justice and righteousness. The message, then, is simply this: After all the care God showered on His people, they failed to live up to

His expectations; therefore He was going to remove His blessings and allow them to be ruined.

WHY COMBINE TWO GENRES?

Why did Isaiah shift to a song to deliver this message? Why not simply present the message as an exhortation? What do we need to know about poetry, psalms, and songs to appreciate what Isaiah is attempting to accomplish?

To go deeper, begin thinking about poetry, a genre that doesn't follow the conventions of logic and makes statements that are true, but not in a technical sense. For example, "the house of Israel" was not a vineyard—it wasn't even a "house," but a nation, a people.

Poetry is not written in the language of the head but of the heart. Poetry communicates with pictures, metaphors, symbols, and figures of speech. The truth we find in poetry is not so much the kind of truth you can prove mathematically, but a truth you *feel.* A song or poem creates a sense of "knowing in your gut."

But why use poetry to deliver this particular prophecy? Perhaps Isaiah wanted to circumvent rational objections and aim right for the heart. Most likely the nature of his message required his readers to *feel* its truth rather than simply acknowledge it. Both emotion and reason drive our decisions and actions. People rationally reflect on what they feel, and we also have feelings about rational ideas or concepts. The two overlap.

WHAT WAS ISAIAH'S GOAL?

If poetry is designed to induce feeling, what did Isaiah want his audience to feel? Perhaps the song was intended to draw them into God's feelings, to give them empathy for God's disappointment. Isaiah not only composed a song, he composed a *ballad,* a song that tells a story. In the story, God is depicted as a very busy farmer: He "dug," "cleared," "planted," "built," and "cut." Most of the people in Isaiah's audience would understand something about the amount of labor implied in each of these activities. The soil of Israel is thin and rocky, especially in the north where much of the land is littered with basalt rocks. Hearing this song, the audience would easily imagine the farmer toiling under the hot sun, clearing his field, and planting his vines. Since he began with a "fertile hillside," he had every reason to expect his intense labor to pay off in an excellent crop. But this crop had a mind of its own.

At this point, God breaks into the song and speaks directly through His prophet. "Now you dwellers in Jerusalem and men of Judah, judge between me and my vineyard" (verse 3). God challenges them to weigh the evidence, to consider the circumstances, and render a verdict. Maybe they have an explanation for the bad crop. Maybe they could tell God what He had failed to do for them. So He asks, "What more could have been done for my vineyard than I have done for it?" (verse 4).

The song leaves them speechless (or assumes they have no response). They could not answer either question. God then speaks again: "Now I will tell you what I am going to do to my vineyard." Once again God will be busy, only this time He will "take away," "break down," "make it a wasteland," and "command the clouds not to rain on it."

DEVICES PECULIAR TO THE WISDOM GENRE

Isaiah makes use of several literary devices common to the Wisdom Literature. But for now let's concentrate on two of them. The first is known as *chiasmus* (from the Greek letter *chi,* or x). The verse (or passage) written in this form will crisscross itself, so that the second line of a sentence reverses the order of the statement in the first line. A chiasmus may look something like this:

John rode off to the library,
And off to the store rode Mary.

Whereas *John* is the first word of the first line, *Mary* is the last word of the second line. This is how the chiasmus looks in the first half of Isaiah 5:7:

The vineyard of the LORD Almighty
   is the house of Israel,
and the men of Judah
   are the garden of his delight.

Where we might expect the order of the second line to follow the order of the first line, it reads backward instead.

The second device in this verse is known as *parallelism,* which can take several forms. The parallelism in this verse is referred to as "synonymous," which means the second line repeats the first line but with different words. So Isaiah says:

And he looked for justice, but saw bloodshed;
   for righteousness, but heard cries of distress.

The words *justice* and *righteousness* are linked, as are the words *bloodshed* and *cries of distress.* Sometimes the use of parallelism helps us understand what Old Testament authors meant by certain words. In this instance we see that *justice* can be a synonym for *righteousness.*

Why bother to look for these devices when we can appreciate Isaiah's message without them? Because the language of poetry draws attention to itself. Poets will sometimes use words in unconventional ways to make us more conscious of what is being said. (Their turn of phrase has been called "an organized violence committed on ordinary speech."[2]) If our everyday speech has become stale, the poet will use a word or phrase in a way that draws attention to itself. For instance, viewing the nation of Israel as a vineyard gave Isaiah's audience a new way of thinking about God's disappointed expectations.

Isaiah wanted his readers to wake up to all the care God had poured into their lives. If the prophet had used direct language, his listeners may not have seen the intimacy and nearness of God, they may have been deaf to God's voice. So the prophet sang about the One he loved. And in the middle of the song, God prophetically broke in and sang the chorus. "You are My vineyard. I designed the circumstances of your life with this purpose in mind, to make you spiritually productive. What more could I have done to bring out the best in you?"

YET ANOTHER GENRE

This passage is not only a song (specifically, a ballad), but it is also a *parable*—a story that depicts a reality other than itself. When Isaiah sings about a loved one, a vineyard, a fertile hill, a winepress, and so on, is he talking about real objects and places? Yes and no. He is not saying that God planted a literal vineyard and built an actual winepress in it. Yet at the same time, the objects mentioned existed somewhere and the actions of the farmer were true to life. Vineyards must be cared for and farmers have to do real work to produce a good crop.

But Isaiah's message and meaning are not about farmers and vineyards. The reality of the song is a message about God's work and the failure of the people. Isaiah's song, in the way it (ab)uses words and pictures, is meant to upset our comfortable reality and point us to another reality. We may be thankful for our prosperity and think the world is just fine, but God calls us over to His side of the street so we can feel what He feels—the disappointment of a failed crop after working so hard to ensure its quality.

Some of the word pictures are almost enchanting. For example, when Isaiah refers to the men of Judah as "the garden of his delight," we naturally see an allusion to the original paradise in Eden. There God and humans enjoyed intimate communication. There was peace between heaven and earth. God had also "planted" the Garden of Eden (see Genesis 2:8), and that lush garden also required tending. We might even follow the Genesis story to its end, in which, like the people of Isaiah's time, human disobedience foiled God's desires for His people. As in the Garden of Eden, so in Israel and Judah: Intimacy with God was displaced by alienation. A close reading of Isaiah's song, with an appreciation for the type of literature we are reading, will help us find these important images.

PUTTING IT ALL TOGETHER

We have only scratched the surface of this beautiful passage, but we are now much closer to its meaning. To develop your own interpretive skills, grab your Bible, draw a line around a favorite passage, and begin to ask the genre questions listed earlier in this chapter. It's a good idea to keep an English dictionary and Bible dictionary close by. If you have any other reference works or any background in the Bible's original languages, you are even more fortunate!

When you ask questions of the text, listen for its answers. Listen also for the "still, small voice" that speaks to you personally through the text. This isn't a mere intellectual exercise; it's the pursuit of God's truth and its application to your life. You now have a new "power tool" (genre) for opening the meaning of Scripture. Use it well.

CHAPTER 3

"AND IT CAME TO PASS"

Paying Attention to the
Elements of Story

Can you think of a story that has had a lasting impact on you? Perhaps it was so sad, frightening, funny, or encouraging that it will always be with you. A good story has the power not only to touch our emotions but to change our lives.

It's true that everybody loves a good story; otherwise you wouldn't have to stand in a long line to buy tickets on the opening night of the latest *Star Wars* episode or Tolkien cinematic saga. But what makes a story a story—as opposed to a report, contract, or essay? Stories are interesting because they are made up of components that enable the reader, or listener, to enter the experience of the characters. This element of personal experience gives stories a special power.

The effort we invest in identifying the elements that comprise a story will be richly rewarded. First, a close reading will help us relate to the characters. The events and ordeals that shaped their lives will become formative in our own lives. Traveling with the main characters will open our eyes to subtle details and occurrences in the text. Second, we will learn to become better storytellers ourselves, enhancing our ability to tell the stories of the Bible. Understanding the elements of story will open our eyes to the deeper truth contained in these stories.

THE UNIVERSAL LANGUAGE

Stories embody the values and aspirations of every culture. They are the primary method of enculturating children into the worldview and customs of their tribe or culture. Even in day-to-day admonition, we invoke brief stories to drive home lessons to our children: "If Joey jumped off a cliff, would *you?*"

If you know a culture's stories, you can learn much about that culture. Numerous stories translate well from culture to culture, even as the ancient stories of the early Greek poets and playwrights still speak to us today. The movie *O Brother, Where Art Thou?*, set in the Depression-era American South, was inspired in part by Homer's masterwork *The Odyssey*, written in the eighth or ninth century B.C. Likewise, ancient stories from Scripture have lost little of their currency. My guess is that Jesus' story of the prodigal son can be easily understood today in almost every culture of the world.

In the first half of the twentieth century, certain scholars produced a theory of language known as *structuralism*. They maintained that language systems formed the basis of culture. However, the structuralist model has been replaced by a new theory: that culture is formed more by *story* than by language, and that language itself is derived in part from stories. Stories are the essential building blocks of culture and community. We learn our first stories during our prelinguistic development as we experience our world through events, and only later do we learn how to articulate those events. Language enables us to put into words the stories we already know.

FINDING TRUTH THROUGH A STORY

Thinkers in the modern era were largely biased against stories as a means of conveying truth. Stories, it was assumed, were too flimsy to satisfy the intellect. Essays and dissertations were thought to be superior for conveying truth, since they rely on facts and appeal to logic and reason. This bias was reflected within the church in the form of expository preaching and the familiar three-point sermon, which took precedence over storytelling. What got lost is the truth that Jesus did the majority of His teaching by telling stories. The Bible itself is more story than anything else.

As long as stories conform to certain rules, there is no reason they can't serve as powerful vehicles for revealing truth. But the rules that govern storytelling are important. For example, a story must have internal credibility: Every event must fit the worldview created by the narrator. If the plot is set in the real world, then one of the human characters cannot suddenly flap his arms and take to the air. However, if the story's characters do fly, then other conventions will determine what can and cannot be done. If the internal credibility of the story breaks down, it takes the form of propaganda and its truth will be lost.

BEARING THE TRUTH

Stories have their own power of persuasion that is independent of the demands of logic. Stories provide illustrations that help the mind grasp abstract concepts or open up the scientific mind to breakthrough inventions. A story may be entertaining but also serve a deeper purpose, such as shaping the worldview of an entire culture. Think of the tide of history being turned when King Rehoboam told the northern tribes of Israel, "My father made your yoke heavy; I will make it even heavier. My father scourged you with whips; I will scourge you with scorpions" (1 Kings 12:14). With that fateful word picture he split the kingdom and destined Israel to a civil war that lasted hundreds of years. In similar fashion, Jeroboam's retelling of the story of Israel's deliverance set the northern empire on an idolatrous decline from which it never recovered (see 1 Kings 12:28-30).

ENHANCING INSIGHT

Stories are a great source of personal insight, because we learn about ourselves even as we read about others. Studying the elements of a story gives us a kind of double vision—we are looking through a window yet also seeing our reflection in the glass. In describing the characters and their circumstances, the story invites us to look at our own lives.

The Christians of the early church—especially outside Judea—did not have anything like a systematic theology available to them. What they had were the stories embodied in the gospel: the life, ministry, teaching, miracles, death, and resurrection of Jesus. Those stories not only formed the beliefs of the church but also carried the truth that introduced people to the life of God (see John 20:30-31).

A POSITIVE AND A NEGATIVE

As we study the stories of Scripture, remember that each story must be taken as a complete unit, thus reinforcing its integrity. In the past, critical scholarship has freely removed passages from the Bible or switched the text around to accommodate what was believed to be a scribal mistake or anachronism. The power and meaning of the story gets lost in the zealous study of context, source material, and other historical details.

In contrast, narrative scholars argue that a text's present form is the *intended* form of the author or scribe. In other words, even if the history narratives found in 1 and 2 Kings come from a variety of sources, the form in which they appear is the form in which they were meant to be read. One of the wonderful qualities of narrative study is that it assumes the integrity of the text. Questions that trouble some students of Scripture are set aside, such as whether the text was written by one author at one time or pieced together by a number of different editors over many years.

Of course, this approach also represents a potential danger if it makes no difference to the reader whether the story is *true* or relates to anything in the real world. But the integrity of biblical stories makes all the difference to Christians. (Many biblical stories were never intended to recount actual events but, as in the case of allegories and parables, serve to make other points.[1])

We will exercise caution when making use of narrative analysis to understand the Bible's message and meaning. Generally we will be safe if we also apply what we know of biblical genre and historical research. Genre will help us determine if the story is meant to be understood as an actual historical event, and if so, historical research will give us cultural and linguistic clues for interpreting the context of the event.

ELEMENTS OF STORY

I still don't know what to think about dissecting frogs in high school biology classes. Even though the cause of science education is served, it occurs at the cost of the frog's life. To study and understand the interior of a frog means a particular amphibian has to die—and I doubt that a frog would gladly exchange its life for the advance of science.

Some people worry that if we open up a story and explore its infrastructure, the story will die, that it will lose something of its energy and power. No doubt, a beautiful narrative can become as dry as desert sand when dissected in a purely academic way. If we pretend to understand all the dynamics of a good story, believing they can be separated from the complete narrative and individually assessed as if in a laboratory, then we have betrayed the soul of story, which aims primarily at the reader's heart.

We can, however, adopt a different attitude that actually releases more of a story's energy and passion as we descend into its core. For example, if we look at all the ways a character is developed, we come to know that person better and form a stronger identification with him or her. If we look for plot clues, we increase our interest in the story even as its theme becomes richer to us. Also, when we engage in a close reading of a story, we are less likely to overlook or misinterpret its meaning.

> ### THE BIG IDEA:
>
> The stories of the Bible were meant to be more than engaging entertainment. The message and meaning of a story become clear when we recognize and understand the storyteller's devices and how they are used.

Every story is made up of four primary ingredients: plot, characters, atmosphere, and tone. These are the basic tools we need for exploring the meaning of a narrative. As you learn to identify these four elements, the narrative will open itself and tell you secrets you've never heard.

THE PLOT

A story has forward momentum because of its plot, the series of events that the writer links together. The plot cannot be a series of random events, such as: John entered the house; a car screeched to a stop outside; Lester ran away shaky but unharmed. These events do not form a story, because the relationship between them is unclear. However, if we are told that John came home to find that the front gate had been left open and his dog, Lester, was not in the yard, then we can see the potential development of a plot. (We *really* start worrying about Lester when we hear the screech of the car's tires.)

The storyteller determines the story's plot. So even though Matthew, Mark, and Luke—and in some cases John—recount some of the same episodes in Jesus' life, they do not always place them in the same sequence or include the same details. Each writer developed the plot of Jesus' story as a way to emphasize the spiritual points he felt were crucial to the essence of the gospel.

A story's plot usually involves tension or conflict that serves to build suspense. Suspense is created when the plot raises questions that the reader expects to be answered later. When those questions have been answered, the tension is resolved—the criminal is arrested, the stolen valuables are returned, the lovers are reunited.

The plot of a story often can be determined by asking: What is the tension in the story that needs to be resolved? Tension often arises from a conflict between two characters or by an ordeal that the primary character must face. The reader hopes to discover whether the hero will make a wise or foolish choice. The tension in the plot often serves to produce a change in the hero or main character so that by the end of the story he has become a different person. (Paul's encounter with Jesus on the road to Damascus is a dramatic example of such a change.)

Several of Jesus' stories demonstrate His awareness of suspense. In fact, He left at least one story unfinished with the suspense unresolved. The story of the unproductive fig tree can be found in Luke 13. The owner of a vineyard noticed that a fig tree he had tended for three years was not producing any fruit. He told his caretaker to cut it down, but the caretaker offered to weed around the tree, fertilize it, and water it for one more year. If it still failed to bear fruit, then it would be destroyed (see Luke 13:1-9).

The suspense in Jesus' story rises from the question: What happened the following year? Did the tree bear fruit, or was it removed and burned? Jesus intentionally ended His story without revealing the outcome. If someone were to ask Jesus what happened, He might say something like, "I don't know. I will examine you for fruit again next year, then we will know." Jesus chose not to resolve the suspense so His listeners would realize it was up to them to determine the end of the story. Would they take this opportunity to repent, or would they put it off?

If you can't locate the tension of a story, it's possible that the plot serves a purpose other than to resolve the suspense. Sometimes a plot aims at enlightenment. In these stories, a character is likely to come across a number of facts that eventually coalesce into the full understanding of a subject or event. This may be the plot of the book of Ecclesiastes, to the extent that it may be considered a narrative (in this case, an autobiographical story). After searching through a variety of life pursuits, the Teacher concludes that everything is "meaningless." The important lessons of Ecclesiastes are the result of the insight and understanding that the Teacher picked up during his quest. The acquisition of wisdom and knowledge, and the conclusion that is reached, make up the plot.

If the story has a message, it emerges from the evolving plot. Whatever the characters learn, we also learn. In fact, we often learn *more* than the characters, because we are given the added benefit of a vantage point from outside their situation.

To uncover the plot, ask the following questions:

• What is the main tension running through the story?
• What is the preoccupation of the main characters? What are they trying to do? What forces oppose them?
• What moves the main characters? What events push their story along?

THE CHARACTERS

A plot is advanced by the story's characters. The characters may be instrumental in producing events, they may be affected by events, or they may be witnesses to events, like the neutral "crowd" that often appears in the Gospels. These people witnessed the conflict between Jesus and the religious leaders, and sometimes they praised Jesus' actions (see Matthew 15:31; Mark 2:7-12; Luke 13:17).

The plot usually involves a main character (the protagonist or hero) whose experiences form the core of the story. Opposing the main character is the antagonist (the enemy or villain) whose scheming helps generate the story's tension. The hero will sometimes have a confidant or sidekick whose presence serves to point out the strengths of the hero. The nervous servant of Elisha serves this role, as did Joshua with Moses (see 2 Kings 6:15-16; Numbers 11:28-30 respectively).

We get to know main characters in several ways: Narrators may describe them to us, their speech and actions reveal their traits, or we may get to know them through their interactions and conversations with others. In each encounter we see a new aspect of their personality.

Sometimes characters experience a transformation before the story ends. Zacchaeus, for example, went from being a miserly tax collector to a generous philanthropist (see Luke 19:1-10). Characters who are capable of change are referred to as *dynamic*. Other characters who cannot change are known as *static*. Caleb, in the Old Testament book of Numbers, is a static character—after forty years he remained the same person, which in his case was a virtue (see Numbers 14:24; Joshua 14:6-12).

Characters also can be either complex or simple. A complex character has a variety of traits and is capable of change—and thereby has the potential to surprise the reader. Complex characters resemble people like us. Because they generally have well-rounded personalities, they are also referred to as *round characters*. In every story about Jesus, He is always presented as a complex character. Most of the disciples are also complex characters—especially Peter, John, and James.

A character who is simple is referred to as a *flat character*. Flat characters have few traits and are predictable and static. Both the Pharisees and the crowds that came to Jesus are flat characters. Only when an individual, like Nicodemus, steps away from the group and exhibits unique traits does he become a round character.

Like simple characters, *stock characters* are not well-rounded and generally exhibit only one trait. As a rule, stock characters represent a universal type of person. If their trait is greatly exaggerated, they become a caricature or stereotype. Stock characters include anonymous shepherds, lepers, soldiers, and so on.

Questions to ask about characters include:

- Who is the main character in the story? Who is the antagonist (if there is one)? Does the main character have a confidant, and if so, how does that person help advance the plot?

- Can you identify round characters, flat characters, and stock characters? Which characters are dynamic and which are static?
- What are the characters' identifiable traits? What clues are given to help us identify those traits? (Hint: The name given to biblical characters is frequently the quickest way to learn their traits.)
- Does the main character affect plot development, or is he affected by the plot?

THE ATMOSPHERE

Stories don't take place in a vacuum. There is a setting, a background, and a set of circumstances that create the atmosphere. When Mark tells us that Jesus entered a synagogue and some of the people were "looking for a reason to accuse Jesus" (3:2), he depicts an atmosphere of conflict and hostility. Jesus then acts against a background of tension, because the mood is so volatile. To miss the mood is to lose an important aspect of the story.

Atmosphere consists of a variety of factors working together to recreate a feeling. The setting, for instance, indicates what the reader should feel. Time, place, and circumstances are also important indicators of atmosphere.

A story's time frame may be in a certain season of the year, an hour of the day, or a period of history. A story "in the days of the Judges" will have a different mood than one that occurred after Israel returned from exile in Babylon. Morning has a different feeling—fresh and hopeful—than evening or midnight. Winter and spring are unique, as are times of planting and of harvest.

Beyond times and seasons, the location also speaks volumes about the mood or feeling. Have you noticed how many people met God in the mountains? Moses and Elijah met God on Mount Sinai. Elijah also met God on Mount Carmel. Peter, James, and John met God on the mountain where Jesus was transformed. As for Jesus, He preached on mountainsides, went up into a mountain to pray, wept on the Mount of Olives, and was crucified on Mount Calvary. Other significant places are deserts, lakes, homes, and the temple.

The circumstances in the setting are important for creating atmosphere. The immediate situation may speak of danger, celebration, or dread. For example, we can imagine the eeriness of Abram's encounter with God when the story is set up with the following words: "As the sun was setting, Abram fell into a deep sleep, and a thick and dreadful darkness came over him" (Genesis 15:12).

We can identify the atmosphere by looking for the following:

- The environment in which the story is set. If the events occur in a boat on a lake, what might that suggest about the mood?
- Consider the time indicators that are provided, including the time of day or the season of the year. What might we expect from a story that begins "In the spring"? (See 2 Samuel 11:1.)
- What circumstances surround the story? That Daniel prayed may speak of his piety, but that he prayed when an edict had outlawed prayer reveals his courage.

THE TONE

Oral language can be sarcastic, lighthearted, despairing, apathetic, friendly, or boring. The same tones can be used in writing a story. The tone is established by the writer's style, grammatical devices, and specific statements regarding the plot or the actions of the characters.

Closely related to tone is *point of view*. The storyteller writes from a particular vantage point. If the storyteller is inside the plot, then personal pronouns will be used (as when Paul told the story of his conversion or the famous "we" passages in Acts when Luke was apparently traveling with Paul). If the storyteller stands outside the plot, then third-person pronouns are used (he, she, they). Most of the Bible is told by a narrator who stands outside the story sometime after the events took place.

The *omniscient* point of view allows the storyteller to speak from God's vantage point. From this perspective, the storyteller can touch on events that took place anywhere and at any time (including the future). The storyteller can also divulge the characters' interior life, exposing their thoughts, motives, and feelings (see, for example, 1 Samuel 15:32).

The storyteller's point of view can get tricky, because the actual narrator is hidden somewhere outside the story. For example, when Abraham sent his servant to find a bride for Isaac, the servant told Laban the long story of his mission and how he met Rebekah (see Genesis 24:34-49). As we read about the servant telling his story, we need to keep in mind that someone else is telling us that the servant is telling his story. The servant is a character and not the narrator.

The tone of the story emerges as the narrator's attitude is expressed in descriptions and use of specific phrases. Sometimes biblical writers don't specify whether a character's behavior was good or bad, but the tone of the story reveals the writer's view. We have to be sensitive to the story's tone to gain a clear understanding of the potential moral lesson.

Look for the tone of the story in the following elements:

- The point of view: Does the storyteller speak in the first person ("I," "we") or in the third person ("he," "she," "they")? Is the story related immediately after the events took place or many years later? Is the point of view omniscient or limited?

- Specific statements made regarding the moral and spiritual nature of the characters, circumstances, or plot.

- Any sort of interpretation within the story that goes beyond a simple report of the facts. For example, when the storyteller informs us, "But the thing David had done displeased the LORD" (2 Samuel 11:27), he provides us with more information than is available in the actual events. The tone of God's displeasure can then be read backward into the earlier circumstances.

- The specific issues and details that are brought into focus by the storyteller. Every story emphasizes some details and briefly passes over others. By observing what receives much attention and what receives little, the tone should become clear.

CASE STUDY: THE BOOK OF RUTH

The Old Testament contains a masterpiece that demonstrates the four elements that make up a story. To tackle the book of Ruth on your own, briefly review the descriptions of plot, character, atmosphere, and tone, then begin reading with those elements in mind. You will have to read the entire book to get a feel for its tone, but the first few sentences will provide you with a good start. When you have finished your work, return to this chapter and read the following brief assessment.

ATMOSPHERE

> In the days when the judges ruled, there was a famine in the
> land, and a man from Bethlehem in Judah, together with his wife
> and two sons, went to live for a while in the country of Moab.
> (Ruth 1:1)

The book's opening sentence tells us a great deal about the time, place, and circumstances. The "days when the judges ruled" was a chaotic period summarized by the last sentence in the book of Judges, "In those days Israel had no king; everyone did as he saw fit" (Judges 17:6; 21:25). We can't imagine a period in which there was greater spiritual darkness.

The second indicator of atmosphere is the reference to a famine, which reinforces the negative mood. Besides the hardship created by the famine, it also represented a spiritual puzzle: What happened to God's blessing? The Promised Land, described in Exodus 3:8 as a land "flowing with milk and honey," had become barren. When God suspended His blessing, it generally meant that He had some specific grievance with His people.

There is a third factor that establishes the atmosphere. A "man" with his "wife and two sons" are thrown into the scene against the background of a dark epoch. We can imagine that their flight from Bethlehem was a difficult choice—to take up residence in an alien country—and entailed much sadness as they said good-bye to their neighbors, friends, and family. The author has created an atmosphere of sadness and despair in the first few lines of the story.

At first, neither the man nor his wife is named, and their anonymity adds an element of depth to the story. They become a generic couple with two sons who bear a resemblance to the original family: Adam, Eve, Cain, and Abel—who were also generic in the sense of being the first man, woman, and siblings. And just as Adam and Eve were forced to flee and survive outside paradise, this man and wife are driven from Bethlehem (which means "house of bread"[2]) to seek subsistence in a hostile, foreign land.

The sad mood will climax in the statement Naomi makes, that "the Almighty has made my life very bitter" (Ruth 1:20). But even as Naomi summarizes the opening episode, the storyteller gives us a preview of the episode to follow and in doing so changes the mood. For when Naomi returned to Bethlehem, it was exactly when "the barley harvest was beginning" (verse 22). The famine that drew a dark cloud over the first scene will be forgotten.

The season of harvest and the themes of fertility, redemption, and restoration will pervade the rest of the story. Thus the dark atmosphere of the first chapter is replaced by a brighter atmosphere that speaks of hope and salvation. The climax of the joyous mood comes with the birth of Naomi's grandson who washes away the grief of the earlier losses. The story ends with the promise of an even greater hope and salvation: The descendants of Naomi's grandson are followed to the illustrious King David.

CHARACTERS

For such a short story, the main characters in the book of Ruth are well developed. It is as if the storyteller is concerned that the integrity of each important character—Naomi, Ruth, and Boaz—is revealed. Each one has virtues that are instrumental in achieving a specific outcome.

The man's name was Elimelech, his wife's name Naomi, and the names of his two sons were Mahlon and Kilion. They were Ephrathites from Bethlehem, Judah. And they went to Moab and lived there. Now Elimelech, Naomi's husband, died, and she was left with her two sons. They married Moabite women, one named Orpah and the other Ruth. After they had lived there about ten years, both Mahlon and Kilion also died, and Naomi was left without her two sons and her husband. (Ruth 1:2-5)

Elimelech and his sons are simple (or flat) characters. The storyteller makes no attempt to develop their personalities or draw us into their personal suffering. They serve more to enhance Naomi's story. Nevertheless, their names are significant. Elimelech means something like "God is King" or "My God is King," which seems ironic given the fact that he settles in the land of a foreign god. Nevertheless, we discover that Elimelech's name is appropriate insofar as God is king in Moab as well as Israel, and He is the eternal king who ordains earthly kings (like David, who comes from Elimelech's bloodline).

Naomi's name is also ironic, at least in the beginning, because it means "pleasant" or "delight." At the end of the first chapter we find Naomi changing her name to Mara, or "bitter" (see also Exodus 15:23), but the name change doesn't really work and she remains Naomi throughout the book—her bitterness was a temporary condition. The destiny of God's people is always to rise above the current moment and live in the light of eternity.

Scholars are pretty much in agreement that Mahlon means "weak" or "sickly," and Kilion comes from a root word that means "destruction," "consumption," or "failing." Their names signal their destiny in the land of Moab. (Within ten years they both were dead.) The dark mood of the days of the judges and the famine in the land hovers over the death of Naomi's men and her subsequent grief.

Nevertheless, since Naomi is a main character, her story will go on. In verse 3 the storyteller hints at Naomi's importance by shifting her position in relationship to Elimelech. In verse 2 she was "his wife," but in verse 3 Elimelech is "Naomi's husband," thus giving her more prominence in the story while preparing the listener for Elimelech's exit.

The names of Orpah and Ruth present scholars with greater challenges. We don't know if these names were derived from the Moabite language or from Hebrew. But apart from the meaning of their names, the important traits of these characters are revealed in their actions. Orpah stays in the land of her people whereas Ruth ventures off to a new land, a new people, and a new God.

> When she [Naomi] heard in Moab that the LORD had come to the aid of his people by providing food for them, Naomi and her daughters-in-law prepared to return home from there. With her two daughters-in-law she left the place where she had been living and set out on the road that would take them back to the land of Judah. (Ruth 1:6-7)

At last Naomi receives some good news: Yahweh "had come to the aid of his people." With no compelling reason to stay in Moab, Naomi prepares to return to Bethlehem. Her Moabite daughters-in-law set out on the journey, no doubt to give her their support. But at some point, Naomi realizes it is not in their best interest (nor hers) for them to return with her. So she pauses on the road to release them of any further obligation, giving them a blessing (see 1:8-9).

Though Orpah is a flat character, she plays an important role. When she decides to return to Moab, she is acting on the wisdom of Naomi's insight and counsel. Like Ruth, she is grieved that her mother-in-law would return to her home, but common sense prevails. Naomi can't guarantee a sunny future in Judah—Orpah would be a foreigner there and perhaps an even greater burden to Naomi. So Orpah "kissed her mother-in-law good-by," expressing her affection for her while parting company.

This sad farewell completes the tragic mood of the first stage of the story, but it turns out to be Naomi's last loss. In fact, the story turns on this very verse. At the same moment Orpah kisses her mother-in-law good-bye, Ruth clings to Naomi. Although Naomi can't see it, her circumstances have already begun to change. While Orpah's decision to stay behind is reasonable, Ruth's decision to travel on is emotional. In light of their circumstances, we would have to say Orpah did the "smart thing," while Ruth was impractical, maybe even impulsive.

When a character in a story acts in a manner that is contrary to her best interest, we have to ask: What is her motivation? The answer is embedded in the story. Ruth will consistently demonstrate her deep devotion to Naomi. At the end of the story, even the women of Bethlehem will remark on Naomi's good fortune to have a daughter-in-law with such excellent qualities (see 4:15).

Of course, we do not need to be told that Ruth loved Naomi. The most profound statement of Ruth's affection comes from her own lips:

But Ruth replied, "Don't urge me to leave you or to turn back from you. Where you go I will go, and where you stay I will stay. Your people will be my people and your God my God. Where you die I will die, and there I will be buried. May the LORD deal with me, be it ever so severely, if anything but death separates you from me." (Ruth 1:16-17)

Virtue shines from every action Ruth performs and every word she speaks. She does not act as an individual consumed in her own needs, but repeatedly demonstrates her concern for Naomi's well-being. Indeed, it is Naomi who is blessed by the birth of Ruth's son at the end of the story (4:14-16). Ruth's interactions with both Naomi and Boaz are characterized by thoughtfulness, tenderness, and intimacy. And whatever kindness Ruth shows to her mother-in-law and future husband is returned to her through their thoughtfulness and generosity.

Naomi is, of course, a complex (or round) character, capable of change. And, in fact, her change is dramatized when she returns home to Bethlehem:

> When they arrived in Bethlehem, the whole town was stirred because of them, and the women exclaimed, "Can this be Naomi?"
>
> "Don't call me Naomi," she told them. "Call me Mara, because the Almighty has made my life very bitter. I went away full, but the LORD has brought me back empty. Why call me Naomi? The LORD has afflicted me; the Almighty has brought misfortune upon me." (Ruth 1:19-21)

The transition involved in a name change was a serious matter for Old Testament men and women. Their names were attached to their identities and destinies. For Naomi to hear her old neighbors call her "Pleasant" was simply too painful—that designation no longer applied. By changing her name she was indicating that the tragic circumstances of her life had redefined who she was. But there are still more changes ahead, and Naomi will once again own her true name.

> Now Naomi had a relative on her husband's side, from the clan of Elimelech, a man of standing, whose name was Boaz. (Ruth 2:1)

The storyteller introduces a new character, although we are not told what role he will play. We are simply told that he was from Elimelech's clan and he was "a man of standing." But the craft of the storyteller is to begin to build suspense, and Boaz will soon be at the heart of it.

As we work our way through this story, we need to pay close attention to the details. Our storyteller is using a device that is similar to what modern moviemakers use: focusing the camera briefly on a specific object—a glove, a cufflink, a coffee cup—without giving any explanation for it. The experienced moviegoer will recognize the importance of that brief closeup as a clue to the plot and will keep it in mind. At this point in Naomi's story, Boaz has no clear role. But we need to keep an eye on him.

From the start, Boaz is depicted as a godly man. His greeting to his harvesters and their friendly response reveal not only a loyalty to Yahweh, rare during the time of the judges, but also a desire to give God a prominent place in their thinking and interactions. We may assume this is Boaz's influence over the workers since he is, after all, their boss. We may wonder if it is only a coincidence that one of the pillars in the temple was named *Boaz* (meaning "strength," 1 Kings 7:21). Boaz is certainly a spiritual pillar in the story of Naomi and Ruth.

Other character elements to note are the stock characters—including the village women (1:19; 4:14) and the elders (4:2)—and the flat character who is never named, yet plays an important role, because he is a closer relative to Naomi and has a prior right to purchase the property that had belonged to Elimelech. Therefore a new element of suspense is introduced (3:18). We should probably try to determine why the storyteller leaves this relative anonymous when names seem to be so important to the other characters.

PLOT

The main tension in the story is this: How will Ruth fare once she has thrown her destiny into her relationship with Naomi? Will her loyalty be her ruin, or will it be rewarded? The challenge is that these women are on their own in a patriarchal culture in which unmarried women are destined to poverty. Ruth does not even have a clan in Judah to watch over her; Naomi has at least that much support.

Suspense builds when Ruth "happens" upon a field owned by Boaz. How will she be treated? Will she be able to collect enough grain to keep her and Naomi from starving? Will the discovery of Boaz's field evolve into a significant plot development?

Suspense builds again when Ruth ventures onto the threshing floor in a gesture that Boaz clearly understands to mean she is available for marriage. Will he be interested in her? Will he take her as his wife? We can even feel his nervousness about the possibility of their being seen together prior to becoming officially engaged (3:14).

Suspense builds yet again when Ruth and Naomi discover there is another relative who has priority in regard to redeeming Ruth along with Elimelech's property—although Naomi appears to be confident that events will turn out in their favor. What if the other relative wants to redeem the field? Will Ruth have to marry this other person, and how will he treat her? It turns out that the relative does want the field, so the suspense is heightened before Boaz pulls out his trump card: To redeem the field entails taking Ruth as his wife and raising a son in the name of Mahlon, her dead husband (see 4:5-10). At this point the final tension is resolved.

There is an underlying plot element that we can't overlook, and that is the work of God going on behind the story. Of course, there are places where His work rises to the surface, as in the blessings and praises peppered throughout the narrative (see 2:4,12,20; 3:10; 4:11-12,14-15). When Ruth decided to join Naomi in her journey home, she also decided to leave the gods of Moab and embrace the God of Israel (see 1:16). In fact, Ruth beautifully exemplifies the theme of redemption. Moabite women were known to be dangerous; they had seduced the men of Israel into sexual sin and the worship of false gods when Israel was still wandering in the wilderness (see Numbers 25:1-3). This affront was not quickly forgotten (see Numbers 31:15-16), and intermarriages with Moabites were forbidden. Ruth, however, is a redeemed Moabite insofar as she is willing to abandon her gods and embrace Yahweh. In joining herself to Naomi and Naomi's God, she becomes eligible for an interracial marriage.

Boaz recognized Ruth's decision and expressed his admiration in a statement that is full of important information:

I've been told all about what you have done for your mother-in-law
since the death of your husband—how you left your father and
mother and your homeland and came to live with a people you did
not know before. May the LORD repay you for what you have
done. May you be richly rewarded by the LORD, the God of Israel,
under whose wings you have come to take refuge. (Ruth 2:11-12)

We could say that the rest of the story is the fulfillment of these words
as God rewards Ruth for her faithful devotion. God is indeed the rewarder
of those who take refuge under His wings.

The story ends with a rather strange epilogue: The genealogy of King
David beginning with Perez (the son of Judah, see 4:12). Nevertheless, the
genealogy gives us an important perspective. We may have wondered why
God put a magnifying glass on this one family from a backwater village.
Certainly their circumstances were difficult and His deliverance and
restoration were wonderful, but does that justify this book's place in sacred
Scripture? The other stories from the period of the judges centered on
people who rose to national prominence, whereas the names of Naomi,
Ruth, and Boaz would never have been known outside this book.

But the genealogy is itself a revelation of God's working through the
ordinary affairs of human lives and moving history to its desired goal. They
were plain, ordinary people—yet God was with them, guarding His will
and promoting their welfare. In some ways, this story of simple people prepares us for the first story we encounter in the next book of the Bible: that
of Elkanah and Hannah. Here are two more people whose lives seem small
and whose grief seems insignificant in the scope of history, yet they play a
crucial role in the establishment of the new, united kingdom of Israel.

TONE

In the book of Ruth, the storyteller adopts an omniscient point of view.
Events move from Bethlehem to Moab and back to Bethlehem without a
break in the story. The reader follows the characters into grainfields, under

a shelter, into the home of Naomi and Ruth, onto a threshing floor, and up to the city gates.

Although the events of Ruth occurred "in the days when the judges ruled," it is impossible to locate a specific time when these events took place. We know *where* precisely, but we do not know when, except that it occurred within a few generations before David. However, not knowing exactly when these events took place may actually be a clue to the tone of the story.

The author wrote the book of Ruth sometime after the events took place, and therefore every conversation is reported in the past tense. Nevertheless, the outcome of the story is hidden from us (and the characters) until the end. Because of the author's perspective, he is able to give us all the relevant details, choosing conversations and events in a way that creates a rhythm and symmetry. This story is a piece of narrative art.

But the storyteller does *not* provide any sort of moral commentary. For example, Elimelech is not criticized for moving his family to Moab; the relative who declined to redeem Naomi's property is not chided for failing to fulfill the obligations of the nearest of kin; and Ruth does not come under fire for her boldness in approaching Boaz on the threshing floor. If we are looking for a moral or spiritual evaluation, it is not to be found. Nevertheless, the storyteller does indicate a value judgment regarding Naomi, Ruth, and Boaz, who are depicted as wise, resourceful, generous, and devoted to the important social and spiritual themes—loyalty to family and to God.

The absence of moral commentary brings to mind other missing elements. For example, there are certain features that mark the book of Judges that we would assume exercised a significant influence over the lives of anyone living during those times. Bethlehem was not far from Zorah, the birthplace of Samson, but the book of Ruth makes no mention of him or any other judge. Other trademarks of the days of the judges are not even hinted at: the direct visitation of angels, the Spirit of Yahweh "coming upon" a judge, the deep tension with pagan deities, and the whole cycle of failure leading to invasion followed by deliverance that recurs throughout the book of Judges.

To sum up the difference in tone between Judges and Ruth, Ruth lacks the dramatic supernatural intervention that followed the charismatic leaders of that era. The writer of this narrative is more interested in the *normal* flow of events in the lives of ordinary people. God is with them, giving meaning to their lives and struggles, invisibly assisting them and rewarding their faith, and by the end of the story God's purposes will be fulfilled not only for them, but on behalf of the whole nation and ultimately the whole world. Ruth was the great-grandmother of King David, whose royal family line produced Mary, the mother of Jesus, almost one thousand years later.

If we are looking for a spiritual lesson—and identifying the story's tone is often a good way to gain spiritual insights—then we find that God is with ordinary people even in the most trying times. Although their experience may be less exciting than the fireworks that erupt with the charismatic judges, their faith, diligence, hard work, and righteousness are guaranteed to be rewarded in the end. This lesson provides tremendous encouragement to other ordinary believers, such as you and me.

CHAPTER 4

THE UNHEARD VOICE

Paying Attention to What
Is *Not* Spoken

I hate to admit it, but most of my political education in the sixties came from pop icons such as Bob Dylan and Randy Bachman of the Guess Who. Simon and Garfunkel were also part of my curriculum. Their classic "The Sounds of Silence" still has the ring of truth for me. In fact, the idea of *hearing* a message from silence—gaining meaning from words that are not said—is also a valuable tool to use in understanding and interpreting Scripture.

In the previous chapters, we paid careful attention to the written words of a text. In this chapter, we'll explore the meaning of information that has been left out, ignored, or excluded. At first, this might seem counterintuitive. Or, as Morpheus said in *The Matrix,* "This will feel…a little weird."[1]

But it's really not all that weird. A great deal of scholarly study consists of filling in the missing pieces. There is hardly a passage of Scripture that doesn't beg for more information. Bible teachers are constantly bombarded with questions like, "Where did Cain get his wife?" "What was God doing prior to creating the universe?" and "Why didn't Lot's wife object when Lot offered their daughters to the men of Sodom?" And these just skim the surface.

THE MYSTERY OF ABRAHAM'S SERVANT

We have much to gain by asking why some information is left out. For example, in Genesis 15:2-3 Abraham made reference to "a servant in his household" by the name of Eliezer. Later on, in chapter 24, Abraham sent his "chief" (or oldest) servant to his native land to find a bride for Isaac. Was this servant Eliezer, and if so, why not mention his name? If it isn't Eliezer, then who *is* this servant? Finding the answers may lead to a significant spiritual insight.

The interesting feature of Abraham's servant is that, even though he remains anonymous in Genesis 24, by virtue of his role and the detailed description of his actions, he eclipses every other character in the chapter. In leaving the servant unnamed, the storyteller defines who he is in the context of his role. He is an important member of Abraham's household who has the temerity to negotiate with his master regarding his mission and has the authority to give away treasures that belong to his master. He finds his identity in faithful service to Abraham, but he also manages to work creatively (and spiritually) within the parameters of his assignment. He may be portrayed as an anonymous servant of Abraham, but we could never say he is unimportant.

The anonymity of Abraham's servant leads to another question: Why are some biblical figures, even a few who play important roles, not identified by name? For example, Nicodemus the Pharisee is named, but in the next chapter of John's gospel the Samaritan woman is unnamed, even though she introduced her entire village to Jesus. Why are we given the name of Rahab the prostitute but not the Israelite spies who promised to protect her? The Bible uses many designations for unnamed characters, including a "wise woman," a "man of God," and a "son of the prophets."

With the understanding that the Bible is inspired by God, we can assume that there are reasons for leaving out certain details. If we want to dig deep into the meaning of Scripture, then we need to carefully consider these omissions. In some instances we will conclude that missing information was irrelevant. But other times we will discover that there were specific reasons for the missing data, and looking for those reasons results in a new and deeper understanding.

THE BIG IDEA:

Leaving out a significant detail is a common storytelling device. Looking for reasons why those details were left in silence takes us deeper into the text.

SEEING WHAT IS NOT THERE

Once, when Jesus was eating in the home of a Pharisee, a "sinful woman" from town entered the dining area and showered Jesus with love. In defending her actions, Jesus pointed out all the things His host had not done for Him: "You did not give me any water for my feet.... You did not give me a kiss.... You did not put oil on my head" (Luke 7:44-46). Jesus found as much meaning in the courtesies His host *failed* to perform as He did in the positive actions performed by the unnamed woman. His host obviously had little love for Jesus compared to the woman who loved Him deeply because her "many sins" had been forgiven.

There are times when behavior, ideas, words, and actions are more noticeable due to their absence. That nine lepers did *not* return to "give praise to God" for their healing was as meaningful to Jesus as the one leper who did express gratitude (see Luke 17:17-18). If you are expecting something to happen, and it fails to materialize, you become more aware of it. Because King Saul expected David to feast at his table during the New Moon celebration, he was especially conscious of the fact that David was missing (see 1 Samuel 20:4-8).

A useful tool for interpreting the Bible is learning to develop expectations about a passage. If we expect it to answer particular questions, provide pertinent information, or explain background details, but the text does not do those things, we can ask, "Why would the Bible exclude this information? What does the silence reveal?"

PEOPLE WITHOUT A VOICE

There are classes of people that the Bible commands believers to protect and nurture. These are people who are constantly in danger of being overlooked, exploited, or oppressed—including widows, orphans, the poor, foreigners, the disabled (see Leviticus 19:14), prisoners of war, and slaves. These people are given rights in the Mosaic law and are granted special consideration in the teachings of Jesus. These people *have no voice* in society. As a class, they have little influence. And as individuals, their grievances or cries for help are rarely heard. Perhaps even in their own town or home they are continually silenced (see, for instance, Mark 10:46-48).

Having a voice is an indication of the existence of a "self" that is capable of reasoning, feeling, and speaking. To be deprived of a public voice is to become a nonentity—a body that may belong to a master or to the state but is not recognized as an independent self. To be denied the power to speak is to be erased as a person.

The Bible seeks to give voice to these people. But there are places in Scripture where a person's voice is not heard. For example, the woman who was caught in adultery and dragged before Jesus did not utter a word as her accusers assailed her. The men who placed her fate in the hands of Jesus did all the speaking. Paying attention to her initial voiceless role and the way Jesus later drew speech from her leads to a beautiful study of His way with people who have been abused into silence.

When we read Scripture with a keen interest in what is left unspoken, we begin to see themes, problems, and conditions that lie just below the surface. When one belongs to a ruling class, it is easy to take for granted the current structure of society. If you don't feel the pain of injustice, you may not realize that society is guilty of silencing entire groups. And if you read the Bible without looking for instances of pain and injustice, you may fail to feel them deeply enough to question your own position of privilege.

When we listen for what is not spoken, we are reading in a way that calls institutions to account for the way they treat people (empires such as Egypt and Babylon), that questions religious authority (the courtly priests and prophets of the Old Testament and the Pharisees and Sanhedrin in the New Testament), that investigates the use and misuse of power and authority (David in regard to Uriah the Hittite in the Old Testament and Herod and Felix in the New Testament). Some people refer to this interpretive method as *subversive*, an accurate description insofar as the Bible intends to destabilize systems that resist God and abuse people. If a nation, corporation, or church engages in activities that oppress people, those activities need to be addressed. A voice needs to be given to those who can't speak for themselves (see Psalm 82:3), but first we must discover who those people are.

Have you ever noticed how many times in the Old Testament a prophet's voice was silenced? Zechariah was executed "by order of the king" when he challenged Judah's disobedience to God (see 2 Chronicles 24:21). King Amaziah ordered an unnamed prophet to stop speaking on the threat of death (see 2 Chronicles 25:16). And, of course, the beheaded John the Baptist comes to mind (see Mark 6:17-28). In each instance, the established political authority felt threatened or undermined by the prophet and therefore eliminated the prophetic voice.

Reading the Bible with an intent to recover the silenced prophetic voice reveals some of the ways that God works to subvert the abuse of power. These insights then become our education in God's view of human society and His concerns for justice, mercy, and faithfulness.

PROCEED WITH CAUTION

When literary critics analyze a text looking for what is not said, they usually have a specific agenda. Deconstructionists attempt to demonstrate how texts collapse on themselves, revealing the absence of meaning. Feminists seek to discover ways in which literature has served to suppress women, how male authors have silenced or excluded women or ascribed to them a subservient role. Marxists wish to draw out the social environment of a text, point out its inherent ideology, how that ideology supports or justifies itself despite its contradictions, and how it undermines social wholeness.

These will not appeal to Christian students because such a predetermined agenda weakens the biblical text. First, the text is weakened because the interpreter's ideology is given priority. The interpreter already has determined what she hopes to find and therefore makes the Bible serve her agenda. Second, these critics do not approach Scripture as the Word of God but as a human composition. They do not look for a divine revelation but for proof of their theories. Third, the Scripture is weakened because it is ransacked for political aims rather than spiritual insight and understanding.

When we look for what lies just below the surface, we have to take care that we don't exaggerate the meaning of silence. There will be times when there is no particular meaning for missing information and other times when information is intentionally hidden. As Moses said, "The secret things belong to the LORD our God, but the things revealed belong to us and to our children forever, that we may follow all the words of this law" (Deuteronomy 29:29). We need spiritual discernment to determine when there is revelation in the omissions as well as in the text. We also need to keep in mind that the Bible carries God's divine authority. We can't go to Scripture looking for confirmation of our pet biases.

To help avoid these traps, we will adhere to certain limits. When we pay attention to what is unspoken, we are not attacking the text, but we are looking at the ways people behave within the text. For example, when emissaries from Gibeon came to Israel with the intent of making a covenant, Joshua and his leaders were suspicious. They asked the emissaries two pointed questions: "Who are you and where do you come from?" The emissaries gave Joshua the evasive answer that they were Israel's "servants" and they came from "a very distant country" (Joshua 9:8-9). If you're following the story as it unfolds, you begin to smell a rat.

Without questioning the reliability of the text, we ask what these emissaries are not saying and why. When we ask why information has been excluded, we are not challenging the motives of the biblical writers, but attempting to go deeper into truth by asking appropriate questions.

In Joshua 9 the emissaries avoid disclosing the details that they are Gibeonites from a nearby Canaanite settlement. As we probe their dialogue, we see deeper into their deception. Perhaps our exploration of the details that the Gibeonites excluded will cause us to become suspicious when people trying to sell us something or talk us into something are evasive in answering our own questions.

ASK THE RIGHT QUESTIONS

The key to discovering deeper layers of meaning consists of learning to ask the right questions. If you have a health-related complaint, your doctor will ask you questions in attempting to make a diagnosis. Your mechanic will also ask specific questions if you complain that your car isn't running well.

Here are the sorts of questions we ask the biblical text when looking for the missing clues:

- **Nameless characters.** If any characters are not given a name, we'll ask, "Why does the storyteller leave this person anonymous?" Is the unnamed person defined by her relationship to others—that is, "mother," "handmaid," "servant"?
- **Speechless characters.** If a character appears in the story but remains silent, we'll ask if that person's voice is suppressed or excluded and why.
- **Missing data.** Are there informational gaps in the story—information that you would expect to be given but that does not appear? If so, explore the reasons why.

- **Lack of resolution.** Does the story fail to achieve resolution? Is the reader left hanging? What sort of an ending would bring a resolution?
- **Prior assumptions.** What sorts of assumptions lie behind the story? These would include assumptions about social and religious status, male and female relationships, master and slave roles, and so on.
- **Someone easily overlooked.** Is there an "other" in the story, even on the margin, or someone who is obviously excluded? An other is neither a main character nor an antagonist but someone who is "different" from the social norm. This could be a slave, foreigner, or leper—a person who could easily be pushed aside.
- **Marginal characters.** How are the people on the margins portrayed? Are we given their point of view? Bear in mind that the Israelites were "marginal characters" in Egypt and later during their exile in Babylon. In those places they were the foreigners and slaves.
- **Finding gaps.** Are there any gaps in space (between places) or time (historical leaps)?
- **Locate the power.** Is there an exercise of power (force) or authority in the story? Who has power and who is denied access to power?

If you travel with these questions for a while, you'll begin to notice missing bits and pieces. You will wonder why scant attention is given to a particular theme or person, and that will lead you on an inquiry resulting in a deeper understanding of the Bible's meaning and perhaps a personal meaning for your life.

CASE STUDY: THE BOOK OF ESTHER

Suppose for a moment that writing a text is like drawing a map. A map contains a number of features that relate one location to another and that define locations according to topography, proximity, and so on. But in determining the boundaries of the map, everything that exists outside is excluded or even treated as nonexistent. Even though we know that other geography exists outside the boundaries of this map, we choose to conceal it. The method of interpretation we are about to apply to the book of Esther strives to make us aware of what has been left off the map. We will be looking at the edges of the map, asking what lies beyond.

The story of Esther begins in the royal palace of the capital city of Persia. King Ahasuerus (his Greek name is Xerxes) had invited his nobles, officials, and military leaders to a feast. The storyteller challenges our credulity by suggesting the king's riches were so great that it took six months to show off all "the vast wealth of his kingdom and the splendor and glory of his majesty" (Esther 1:4). The grand tour was followed by a seven-day banquet in which wine flowed freely.[2]

On the seventh day, King Ahasuerus was feeling the effects of the wine, which may be the storyteller's way of hinting at the king's poor judgment and preparing us for the temper tantrum that followed. Under normal circumstances a king's harem was never seen by anyone but the king and the eunuchs and chambermaids who served him. But on this occasion, having run out of treasures to show off, the king decided to summon Queen Vashti "in order to display her beauty." The queen, however, refused the king's command, which infuriated him. This episode set off a chain of events that resulted in Esther's replacing Vashti as queen. With the Jews in Persia in jeopardy of being wiped out in an act of ethnic cleansing, Esther was now in a position to act in their defense.

THE MISSING VOICE

Let's begin our detective work by asking what is missing from the story. Surprisingly, *God* is missing! Nowhere do we find any mention of God or His personal name. (This is not true, however, of the later Greek text that added narrative comments and dialogue that is included in *The Jerusalem Bible*.) This omission in itself has placed the book of Esther in a precarious position—does it even belong in the Bible? But once we conclude that Esther has a rightful place in Scripture, then we have to wonder why there is no mention of God, prayer, or the temple (although there is a reference to fasting).

Perhaps God is not mentioned because the events in this story took place during the Jewish exile in Persia. There were many Jews who felt abandoned by God, forgotten and forsaken (see Lamentations 5:20). God had not relinquished His sovereignty over the world, but He had turned His back on Israel (see Jeremiah 18:17). Removed from their homeland, settled into a foreign country under the rule of a pagan king, and exposed to heathen idols, Israel felt far from God.

It's possible that one of the lessons of the book of Esther is to teach God's people how they are to conduct themselves when He withdraws and silences the prophetic voice. "We are given no miraculous signs; no prophets are left, and none of us knows how long this will be" (Psalm 74:9). When the Israelites are exiled from their land, will they be able to maintain their identity as a people? Will they preserve the solidarity of their community? Will they stay loyal to their faith, their traditions, and their culture? If they are to retain their identity, then how? The story of Esther demonstrates how God's people remain His people when He has withdrawn His presence and when they live in exile.

It is important to note that not only is God's name not mentioned, His voice is excluded from this dramatic story as well. Perhaps the storyteller is helping the Jews in exile to discover how God identifies with them, that He joins them in their unvoiced oppression and suffering. For in the book of Esther, the Jewish people have no voice other than to celebrate and rejoice. But not even the lyrics of their songs (psalms) are recorded.

Unlike the book of Exodus, where God heard the "cry" of the children of Israel and "spoke" to Moses, in the book of Esther both God and His people are silent. God joined Israel, the silenced people, and even in His voluntary silence He communicates His union with them. In this way the

Jews learned they were not alone in their affliction, that "In all their distress he too was distressed" (Isaiah 63:9). The absence of God from the courts of King Ahasuerus actually indicates His presence and solidarity with Israel.

Consider another point: In not mentioning the name of God, the storyteller makes God's role even more noticeable. Esther "was lovely in form and features" (2:7), but who made her so? Mordecai happened to overhear an assassination plot, but his service to the king was forgotten until a providential moment. Who troubled the king's sleep and gave him the idea to have someone read to him from the royal archives (in the hope that it would put him to sleep)? If Mordecai and Esther wondered if she had "come to royal position for such a time as this" (4:14), it is because they recognized a will other than their own at work. God may not be mentioned and He may not speak, but His presence and work are evident.

Perhaps we hear faint echoes of God's voice as He speaks through people. For example, the "who knows?" of Mordecai seems like an attempt to discern God's voice (4:14). It seems also that the words of Haman's wife, Zeresh, and his advisors reflect God's prophetic voice when they predict Haman's downfall (6:12-13). We may also hear at least a whisper of God's voice in the edicts published by the king announcing the good news of salvation to the Jews. Though God may not be personally credited, still He is not completely silent.

God and Israel are not the only characters without a voice. One other important person who is left speechless is Queen Vashti, whose defiance against the king and subsequent removal from her royal position open the way for Esther's rise. Vashti not only occupies a central role in the story, but her refusal to appear before the king and his guests is so significant that we would expect to hear the words she used to turn him down.

Is there any significance in the fact that Vashti's words are not reported? In attempting to answer this question we need to take in the context of the whole first chapter. Then we can see how Vashti, in her wordless protest and banishment, symbolizes Persia's power to exploit, abuse, and silence whomever it chooses.

As we have seen, King Ahasuerus "displayed" his vast wealth for 180 days. Then, during the feast, he sent for Vashti "in order to display her beauty" (in both cases the same Hebrew word is used for "display"). The king regarded his wife on a par with the other ornaments of his kingdom. Some rabbinical scholars have suggested that the king commanded the queen to appear wearing *only* her crown, reducing her to the status of a beautiful trophy. It's possible that Queen Vashti's refusal to appear was not an unwillingness to surrender to the will of her husband but a protest against being regarded as an object.

The reaction of the king's advisor would be comical if it didn't carry such drastic consequences. When Memucan addresses the king, we hear the voice of paranoia exaggerating Vashti's behavior. The use of hyperbole undermines the veracity of the advisor's argument. His (over)use of the word "all" in 1:16-20 (three times in verse 16: "all the princes" and "all the people" in "all the provinces" [KJV]) reveals the danger and chaos he envisions. In his paranoid imagination, every married woman is liable to throw off her husband's authority so that "there will be no end of disrespect and discord" (verse 18). He stops short of saying, "O King, we have a good thing going here. We're able to treat our wives as if they are our property. But if they ever catch wind of Vashti's insubordination, they'll get the notion that they don't have to wait on us hand and foot. Our whole way of life will be destroyed!"

What is missing in Memucan's speech? The very thing the king asked his legal experts to cite for him; that is, a ruling "according to the law" of what should be done to Vashti. Judging from Memucan's response, we may surmise that no Persian law applied to this case. But the king's advisors were not about to let that stop them. In the absence of a legal precedent, they adopted a policy born out of fear.

We might wonder why they chose such a harsh punishment. Obviously they felt threatened by the queen's conduct, but what was the nature of the threat? Memucan warned that "the queen's conduct will become known to all the women" (verse 17). If that were the case, then why not issue a decree that the queen's behavior not be spoken of on pain of death? Why not give the queen some other, milder reprimand? Simply this: Vashti had to be banished from the king's presence, because if the punishment were less severe, she would pose a threat to male dominance.

The banishment is reemphasized in a subtle way. Vashti asserts herself as an independent person, but she is denied the last word. In fact, she is denied *any* words. She enters and exits the narrative, rocking the royal court without uttering a word. And in her banishment, the king's advisors guarantee that her voice will remain silent.

Vashti's silence calls into question the proceeding that deprived her of her throne. The king had a custom of consulting his legal experts "in matters of law and justice," but the case at hand was a domestic dispute. The king's counselors were only too willing to turn it into a legal matter, one that would strengthen their own dominant position with their wives. What does this say about the nature of marriage and the relationship of the sexes if husbands have to continuously silence women in order to maintain control? Male leadership is rather tenuous if it is so easily threatened.

Did the storyteller see a different relationship between the sexes in Hebrew and Persian culture and therefore poke fun at the hysteria Vashti's defiance caused among the king's advisors? (There are times when the only weapon the downtrodden have against their oppressors and the only solace they have against their grief is satire.) As far as being representative of Hebrew culture, Esther certainly followed Mordecai's instructions, "as she had done when he was bringing her up" (2:20). But she was also a self-determining person who was forced to make hard decisions, to act on behalf of her people, to face a mortal enemy, and to exercise power over a nation. In fact, at one point—after Mordecai had applied emotional pressure to convince her to risk her life—Esther turned the tables on Mordecai and gave him instructions, all of which he "carried out" (see 4:15-17). We can be sure that the Hebrews did not advance the cause of women's rights, but there is one aspect of feminine empowerment they consistently practiced, and that was their sincere respect for the call of God. If God called a woman into any field of service, she was respected and obeyed with the honor and submission accorded to any man in the same office.[3]

A STUDY IN CONTRASTS

The silence of Vashti is crucial to the plot of the story because it creates a stark contrast with the good fortune that follows Esther. As a woman deprived of her royal power, Vashti prepares the way for the reader to encounter Esther, who must work within the same cultural constraints, but by the end of the story she is writing decrees with the authority and power of the king (see 9:32). Vashti and Esther are a study in contrasts.

Whereas Vashti is silenced, Esther *cannot* remain silent ("If you remain silent at this time…you and your father's family will perish," 4:14) and is forced to speak, both by circumstances and by Mordecai. When Vashti leaves the story, she is powerless—she acts defiantly but is unable to effect any social change. Esther, on the other hand, is able to undermine male authority (Haman, for example), and the effect is felt worldwide. Vashti's risk lay in the fact that she refuses to appear before the king when summoned, whereas Esther's risk is to approach the king without being summoned (4:11; 5:1-2). Vashti's defiance makes the king furious, but Esther's initiative pleases the king.

Other underlying themes in the early part of Esther fade out by the end, and if we were pursuing an in-depth study, we'd want to know why. One example is the role of wine in scenes where the king makes important decisions. It was when he was "in high spirits from wine" that King Ahasuerus ordered Vashti to appear (1:10). After he accepted Haman's proposal to exterminate the Jews, they "sat down to drink" (3:15). After having a few drinks at Esther's first banquet, he promised to fulfill her request, "even up to half the kingdom" (5:5-6). Wine also played a role in the last feast when the "king got up in a rage, left his wine and went into the palace garden" (7:2,6-8). But wine is not mentioned in any of the subsequent episodes and does not play a role in the king's negotiations with Esther and Mordecai. Is the storyteller making a point through showing wine in a prominent light and then dropping it? Perhaps through further study and meditation you may arrive at a plausible answer that is missing from the puzzle.

Surprisingly, the book of Esther does not end with a final note about the brave and beautiful queen, but about Mordecai who was "preeminent among the Jews, and held in high esteem by his many fellow Jews, because he worked for the good of his people" (10:3). Esther spoke up on behalf of the Jews, but Mordecai receives the praise.

By listening to the silent voices, we have learned that justice and righteousness often reside with those who are silenced or banished, and that God Himself stands among those who have no voice. If Esther disappears from the last chapter, it is not because she is forgotten, but having served her people she now rejoins them as they wait for God's salvation. We have seen that the sounds of silence don't mean we've been forsaken by God, but that He joins our ranks until the time of exile has ended. Like Queen Esther in the final chapter, He silently joins His people in their silence.

WHAT DOES THE

BIBLE DO?

Paying Attention to Your
Own Reactions

In 1971 and 1972 I lived in the town of Twenty-nine Palms, California, "Home of the World's Largest Marine Corps Base." While there, I made friends with a navy corpsman and his wife.

One night during dinner he asked what I thought of a certain song, a popular ballad from the sixties. As I listened to the music, my friend stopped his cassette player after the first stanza, then gave a detailed analysis and interpretation. It took forever to get through the song, with all the starting and stopping. But by the end he had laid out a detailed interpretation that demonstrated that the lyricist had encoded a complicated message about God, salvation, and the Christian faith. I couldn't arrive at all the connections that my friend made, but I was impressed with his enthusiasm and cleverness. The song—perhaps the one song of the twentieth century subjected to more interpretation than any other—was "American Pie" by Don McLean.

Another industrious interpreter of "American Pie" provides a convincing analysis on his Web site, demonstrating that the song carefully, albeit cryptically, documents the tragic death of Buddy Holly, Ritchie Valens, and Jiles P. Richardson (a.k.a. the Big Bopper) in a tragic plane crash in 1959. There are many who subscribe to this interpretation, but are they right?

Cecil Adams writes a column in the *Chicago Reader* in which he answers questions that have been bugging people for a long time. He dedicated one of his columns to the public's fascination with the lyrics to "American Pie." Don McLean later responded in a letter to Adams. He said many people had asked him for an interpretation of "American Pie," but that he felt songwriters should simply make their statements and move on, maintaining a dignified silence.

According to hearsay, when asked by one fan what his song meant, McLean replied, "It means I never have to work again if I don't want to."

In this instance, the songwriter removed himself from the challenge of interpreting his own song. Since we can't read the mind of an author, we can't know his or her intention unless it's stated in the text. In the case of "American Pie," one person can interpret the text in such a way as to find Christian themes while another finds a detailed account of a historic Iowa plane crash. Could McLean have intended both interpretations, neither interpretation, or is it possible he unconsciously encoded more meaning in his lyrics than even he realized?

If an author chooses not to divulge his intention, and if the text fails to convey the intention, then the burden of finding the meaning falls to the readers. How readers go about interpreting a text and the type of interpretations they produce depend on a number of factors, including their personal backgrounds, life experience, and education. What we find depends a lot on what we expect to find, what we have been trained to find, and what we are capable of finding.

Even when the author does reveal his intention—as in Jude 3: "I felt I had to write and urge you to contend for the faith"—the stated intention does not necessarily help us interpret every element of the text. We may have the author's central theme, but we still have to work through the details. Regardless of what the author intended, the reader will find a meaning that makes sense to him.

Here's something obvious that needs to be kept in mind: At the moment someone receives a message, he is in a *situation*—a set of circumstances, a mental state, and so on—and to be in that situation affects the way he hears or receives what is communicated. For example, Jesus once warned His disciples to be careful of "the yeast of the Pharisees and that of Herod" (Mark 8:15). This warning was followed by much discussion among the disciples. One of them found a meaning for the "yeast" reference: "It is because we have no bread" (verse 16). Jesus was able to correct their misinterpretation, but it's obvious that their first attempt to interpret the message was controlled by their situation.

Consider how different situations can affect the way people read and interpret the same text. One person reading the story of David and Bathsheba (2 Samuel 11–12) may belong to a class that is considered "racially inferior" in its host culture. They identify with Uriah the Hittite as the "other" who was betrayed and killed by King David. Another person who is living immorally may be struck by David's sexual sin, the violation of God's commandment, and the punishment that followed. Another person who has a leadership role in a church may take special interest in the way David abused and misused his authority as king. Someone else, who is interested in the charismatic characters of the Old Testament, may focus his attention on Nathan and the creative way he spoke prophetically to the king. Each reader's situation influences his or her interpretation.

Suppose a group of ten readers studies the same passage and each person comes up with the same interpretation, even with an enigmatic text like the following:

"I tell you, on that night two people will be in one bed; one will be taken and the other left. Two women will be grinding grain together; one will be taken and the other left."

"Where, Lord?" they asked.

He replied, "Where there is a dead body, there the vultures will gather." (Luke 17:34-37)

How is it possible that each person could interpret these verses independently and produce the same meaning? It is possible only if they all use the same interpretive method or share a similar situation at the time they read the passage. People who share a similar situation are said to belong to an *interpretive community*. People within an interpretive community—such as a church, Bible college, or religious subculture—share common notions about written texts.

But there is a second powerful influence on interpretation. Have you ever encountered a verse or passage and realized that you interpret it very differently today than you did several years ago? What changed? You are now in a different *situation*. As situations change, interpretations may change as well.

This points to the crucial role of the reader in the discovery of a text's meaning. If we want to learn how to interpret the Bible, we dare not ignore the reader.

THE READER'S EXPERIENCE

Let's assume that authors write with a desire to produce an effect in the readers—emotionally, intellectually, or spiritually. In that case, the passage is structured to evoke a response. One way to read a passage is to take it one word, or one line, at a time, paying attention to how your response develops and changes through the course of the text. This interpretive method is known as *reader response* or *reception theory*. One reason I enjoy this method is because the text is new every time I read it, since my circumstances change from one reading to the next.

To pay attention to our reactions, we need to slow down so that we take in each word as it comes. There are times when the words of one sentence seem to lead the reader to an assumption, only to turn back around in the next sentence and lead somewhere else. We may be surprised by Jeremiah's words, "Moab will be praised" when we know that God had a grievance against Moab. But the next words read, "no more" (Jeremiah 48:2). In a previous chapter, God summoned the Egyptian army to prepare for battle. But in the next verse, the terrified warriors are running from the battlefield (see Jeremiah 46:3-5). God told Isaiah to announce to the people of Israel that they were to "be ever hearing, but never understanding; be ever seeing, but never perceiving" (Isaiah 6:9). This shows us that the text can reverse direction even within the same sentence.

THE BIG IDEA:

The reader's encounter with the text evokes responses that, if taken seriously, can lead to the discovery of new insights that don't emerge when using other interpretive methods.

Some passages in Scripture are confusing, frustrating, or disturbing. Jesus' instructions that "if your right hand causes you to sin, cut it off and throw it away" (Matthew 5:30) has upset many. Even in His own time, would-be followers were put off by Jesus' "hard teaching" (see John 6:60,66). Christians who are disturbed by certain passages are too quick to ask for help in resolving their discomfort. It's possible that discomfort is exactly what the reader is supposed to feel. Maybe our emotional response is what the author intended.

If we pay attention to how the text affects us, then we become aware of how it touches our soul. To do this, we have to become less objective and more subjective. It requires that we travel with the text as if it were a tour guide and we are reacting to the sites that are pointed out to us.

Take Psalm 1, for example:

Blessed is the man that walketh not in the counsel of the ungodly, nor standeth in the way of sinners, nor sitteth in the seat of the scornful. But his delight is in the law of the LORD; and in his law doth he meditate day and night. (Psalm 1:1-2, KJV)

The first word we encounter, "blessed," opens up a world of ideas. We remember that God blessed the first man and woman and told them to be "fruitful and increase in number" (Genesis 1:28). We read of the blessings of God on the lives of people like Abraham and David. We think of His blessings of fertility on the people of Israel (Deuteronomy 7:13). God's blessings are both material and spiritual, and the first word of this psalm promises to divulge the way of blessing.

We then read, "...is the man that walketh." The key to blessing has to do with walking, and again many ideas occur to us. God walked in the Garden of Eden (see Genesis 3:8). Both Enoch and Noah "walked with God" (Genesis 5:24; 6:9). God also walked in the camp of the Israelites and so made Himself accessible to them (see Leviticus 26:11-12). Perhaps we are beginning to get excited about the idea of a spiritual journey and the intimacy of walking with God.

But if we assume the key to blessedness is a matter of walking with God, the psalm surprises us and turns in the opposite direction. The critical factor is that we *do not* walk, and the blessing is for those who "walketh *not*." If the poet is not talking about walking with God, what then? People who want to be blessed are *not* to walk, or follow, "counsel." Here is another surprise, because counsel is highly valued in the Old Testament. Apparently, when it comes to the life of blessedness, counsel is problematic. We read on and discover it is the counsel of "the ungodly" we are to avoid. Naturally this makes sense to us, but we should not forget the process we went through to arrive here. Our "walk" is not the problem, nor is "counsel." The danger comes in the form of ungodly counsel, and to walk in that path is to forfeit God's blessing.

For a reader to monitor his responses to a text, he needs a knowledge of literary devices. Since everything in the text counts, the reader needs a broad understanding of the facets of literature. He also must be willing to abandon early assumptions about the meaning of a text in order to follow it through to the end.

OBVIOUS PROBLEMS

Perhaps our greatest concern with applying the reader-response method of interpretation is the stress it places on the reader rather than on the text. We want to find a stable text in the Scriptures, because from it we derive the truth of God. If the text becomes subject to our reactions, some would be tempted to assume that the truth changes with our changing situations.

From the beginning of this book I have stressed the authority of the Bible and its priority over our interpretations. The truth of God, no matter how dimly we may see it now (see 1 Corinthians 13:12), is eternal and unchanging. God's truth is revealed in Scripture and upheld by the church (see 1 Timothy 3:14-15). What is changing and improving is not the truth but our understanding of it and our relation to it.

Another concern is that if we allow for an interpretation that is as subjective as I have described, does that mean every text is capable of numerous valid interpretations because those interpretations reflect the reader's honest response? I have heard any number of bizarre interpretations based on a person's experience. I've also noticed a number of believers who bend the Scriptures to fit the contours of their desires, emotions, or agenda.

Although several interpretations of one passage are possible, we can't say that *any* interpretation is possible or that all interpretations are equally sound. We cannot inject a meaning into Scripture that is not there already. Our intent is to experience the meaning that already lies in the Bible. We want to *feel* the emotion that the text was meant to evoke. The best safeguard is not to employ this interpretive method apart from other methods of interpretation—in fact, this method demands that we borrow from the other methods as much as possible. Still, there are insights that we won't be able to unlock apart from allowing the text to do to us and in us what it was meant to do.

RESPONDING TO THE TEXT

Paying attention to our reactions won't work well for every passage. However, some sections of the Bible—especially poetry—will come to life as we seek to experience the meaning. So how can we tell if a passage would open well to this type of interpretation? The following clues will guide us:

Do we feel uncomfortable? If something about the text is disturbing, confusing, or frustrating, we should scrutinize our reaction and try to determine its cause. Too often we avoid confronting the feelings the Bible evokes in us. By paying attention to those feelings, we may discover a deeper meaning.

If you have a strong reaction to a text, ask yourself, Why do I feel *this* way? Is this the reaction I'm supposed to feel? It's common for narratives to contain some sort of conflict or tension. Our concern now is not the tension within the narrative, but tension you feel inside after reading the text.

Do we feel expectant? If the events in the passage or the way the text is organized creates an expectation for a particular kind of resolution, then we should consider applying this interpretive method. Anything that leads us along the text in anticipation of what is to follow is eliciting a response that bears reflection.

If you find yourself expecting a certain outcome or development, ask the following questions: What significance does each word hold for my life, apart from a dictionary definition? When I look at the first word in a sentence, what expectations does it raise?

Do we feel unsatisfied? An incomplete story, an unfinished thought, anything that leaves us hanging can cause us to ask what the passage is meant to *do*. (For a powerful example, see a confusing incident in the life of Elisha later in this chapter.)

If you feel unsatisfied after reading a passage, ask yourself: What exactly is missing, and why would the writer intend for me to have that feeling? What is the application to my life of this unfinished story or incomplete thought?

Do we feel whipsawed? If the movement of the text suddenly reverses direction, pay close attention. When Jesus told the disciples that the greatest person in the kingdom was the servant of all, or when He washed their feet even though He was their Master and Lord, He turned upside down our customary notions of leadership, authority, and honor. Such reversals call for deeper exploration.

If you're beginning to feel dizzy or disoriented from a sudden about-face in the text, ask yourself: What is the movement in the text that surprises me? What makes it so surprising? Is this a welcome surprise or a disturbing turn of events?

Do we sense a gap? If we have the feeling there is a gap in logic or some other connection we would expect to find linking one concept to another—then it is up to us to bridge those gaps. It's more difficult to identify what is missing than to notice the elements that are in plain sight. If you feel something is missing, ask yourself: Is there anything here that disappoints or troubles me? If so, is my reaction due to a missing component?

As we monitor our reactions, remember that the goal is to bring together the events and experience of the text in its historical setting and our own contemporary situation. Our goal is to connect the truth of the text to our lives in the world today. Look for what God is saying to you, personally.

CASE STUDY: "GO ON UP, YOU BALDHEAD!"

Let's apply this new tool to one of the most problematic passages in the Old Testament. It's an encounter between Elisha, one of God's most highly regarded prophets, and a group of young children. As you read it, begin to be aware of how you are responding to this episode.

> From there Elisha went up to Bethel. As he was walking along
> the road, some youths came out of the town and jeered at him.

"Go on up, you baldhead!" they said. "Go on up, you baldhead!" He turned around, looked at them and called down a curse on them in the name of the LORD. Then two bears came out of the woods and mauled forty-two of the youths. And he went on to Mount Carmel and from there returned to Samaria. (2 Kings 2:23-25)

This short passage occurs at the end of a series of miraculous events beginning with Elisha taking up the mantle (cloak) of Elijah and slapping the waters of the Jordan River which "divided to the right and to the left" so he could cross over (2:14). Having been given a "double portion" of Elijah's spirit (2:9), Elisha had become a wonder-working prophet of the highest magnitude. A "company of the prophets" who lived in Jericho treated Elisha with honor and respect (2:15). They considered Elisha their master-teacher in prophetic ministry and the leader of their community.

"From there Elisha went up to Bethel" (2:23). Elisha was on the move, perhaps making a circuit through some key villages. Bethel (literally "house of God") was known as a sacred site. Elisha was going about his business, carrying on the ministry of Elijah.

We might pause to reflect on what we feel about this story so far and what we would expect to follow. Wrapped in Elijah's mantle, the prophet seems to move with boldness and confidence. Certainly the people who had known the amazing biography of Elijah and the miraculous stories connected to his name would welcome Elisha. Our expectation: Elisha will be perceived as a man of God and the next great spiritual leader.

"As he was walking along the road" (2:23). Under normal circumstances there should have been nothing eventful about Elisha's journey from Jericho to Bethel, certainly nothing to write about. Therefore we are alerted to the fact that something out of the ordinary is about to happen. Cities and villages, vineyards and mountainsides are the usual sites where important events take place in First and Second Kings. We expect the narrative to pick up at Bethel or some other meaningful place. That the story-

teller draws our attention to Elisha's travels "along the road" draws us deeper into the text.

"Some youths came out of the town" (2:23). No specific town is mentioned so we can't immediately evaluate the character of these "youths." If they belonged to a notorious clan or city, then we could perhaps predict their behavior. As it is, we have to wait to find out how they fit into the story.

The *New International Version's* vague reference to them as "some youths" may be an attempt to tone down what is to follow. True, the Hebrew word *na'ar* can refer to a youth anywhere from an infant to a young man (even one who is married and has children of his own) and is used many times in the Old Testament in contrast to "old." But our storyteller adds the adjective *qatan,* which is a diminutive meaning "to be small or young." When used in relation to other siblings, this term can simply mean the "younger brother." But in this case there are only the children, and they are described as small or young. We would like to think of these children as juvenile delinquents or teenage gangsters, but the language also can mean exactly what the *King James Version* says: "little children."

"And jeered at him" (2:23). If these words fail to surprise us with the appalling rudeness of these children, it is only because we are unfamiliar with Old Testament culture. Israel was not only a patriarchal society, but it was a society that practiced a strict tradition of respect for adults by children, and the elderly by everyone. We can understand the playfulness of children, but this behavior had a cruel edge to it. Rather than the honor we expected Elisha to receive, he is ridiculed.

"Go on up, you baldhead!... Go on up, you baldhead!" (2:23). We don't know exactly what to make of their command "Go on up." Perhaps they mean for him to go on up the road or simply to keep going. Maybe they mean for him to go on up the hill. Some commentators suggest that they mean to go on up into heaven as Elijah had (see verse 11). But there is no doubt about the malice in the appellation "You baldhead!"

Some readers will find this taunting song comical. "It's a big man who can laugh at himself," we say. Children have a way of noticing the obvious and generally lack the inhibition that would prevent them from making such an insulting comment. So at this point there may be readers who are amused by the children's antics.

But other readers will feel quite differently. When researching the subject of baldness as a background for this text, I came across a Web site that posts quotes from men regarding their feelings about losing their hair.[1] Several men admitted they had considered suicide as an alternative to the shame of being bald. Others talked about how they avoided mirrors or even looking at their reflection in windows.

Baldness—at least the male pattern variety—is not something a person can control. Although baldness is a normal occurrence, bald men represent a minority of the male population. Their baldness puts them outside the mainstream.

In biblical times there may have been a concern that baldness was a disease, although Moses assured Israel that the bald man was "clean" (see Leviticus 13:40-41). However, as a sign of grief a man might shave his head (see Job 1:20), as would Nazirites at the consummation of their vow (see Numbers 6:18). Otherwise there was no stigma attached to baldness other than the embarrassment to the individual who, as the Greek doctor Galen observed, might suffer in both appearance and health.

The children did not say, "Go on up, you baldhead!" just once, but twice (and maybe even more times). But a bald man does not need to be taunted more than once to feel utter humiliation. When we read the text with this in mind, we feel empathy for Elisha and a flush of his embarrassment might even wash over us.

"He turned around, looked at them" (2:24). We expect Elisha to keep walking and ignore the taunts. After all, his concerns are wrapped up in the big themes of his nation and their God. And those teasing him are only children. What do they know? But he stopped to look at the children. Again our curiosity is aroused. Was he sizing them up? Was he giving them the "look"?

"And called down a curse on them" (2:24). This is shocking. The great prophet responded to their jeering with a curse. Retaliation seems uncharacteristic of a man of his stature. And a curse is a powerful weapon, one the children could not defend themselves against.

"In the name of the LORD" (2:24). The addition of this line jolts us, because it brings the nature of Elisha's curse to another level. He was not simply rebuking the children or threatening them. He was actually calling on Yahweh to punish them. If we didn't know better, we would think he was committing some form of blasphemy. Why did he resort to such a severe action?

"Then two bears came out of the woods and mauled forty-two of the youths" (2:24). This must be the low point in the story. Not only did God's prophet stoop to cursing children in God's name, but God responded to Elisha's curse. We now feel that God is implicated in something that is morally reprehensible.

"And he went on to Mount Carmel and from there returned to Samaria" (2:25). This is as shocking as Elisha's earlier behavior. The children were mauled by the bears, and the prophet resumed his travels. We wonder how he can return to serving God and his nation after committing such a heartless act.

This story has caused many readers intense discomfort. We may feel disappointed or angry with both the prophet and God. We may feel disgusted with Elisha's behavior and the fact that God stood behind the prophet's curse. What are we to do with this strong sense of discomfort?

Over the years both liberal and conservative scholars have tried to remove the discomfort by attempting to resolve or dissolve the tension. Some liberals have suggested that this story is unworthy of Scripture and should never have been included. Conservatives generally try to rework the text so that the children are teenage thugs who were old enough, and wicked enough, to deserve a good mauling. Then, like Elisha in the text, the commentators simply move on.

Ironically, these scholars are helping us avoid the very thing we are supposed to experience. What if the text was meant to shock us? We expect biblical texts to teach us lessons and round out our knowledge. But the Bible also leads us to *feel* things. If we only have cognitive encounters with Scripture, we won't develop into fully mature Christians. When the Bible forces feelings upon us or evokes emotions, we will grow much more from paying attention to those reactions than if we shut them off.

When we read this text, our discomfort should move us more deeply into the details, to reconsider whether our initial interpretation was correct. We need to unlock our minds from the cage of a single point of view; we need to become more creative, to change our field of reference.

Assuming that the storyteller had a good reason for including this episode, it is very possible that the reason is in the story itself. As a matter of fact, there is a valuable moral in this story, and it has nothing to do with showing respect to elders. So let's find that moral.

The tension in the text arises when the children called out, "Go on up, you baldhead!" Apparently there was some concern about the cause or meaning of baldness in Old Testament times, because Moses had to reassure the people of Israel, "When a man has lost his hair and is bald, he is clean. If he has lost his hair from the front of his scalp and has a bald forehead, he is clean" (Leviticus 13:40-41). Baldness is not a disease; it is simply an unwanted genetic trait. But it is also an alteration that sets a person apart.

This story is about people who are *different,* people who don't fit the norm. This is a story about people whose looks, actions, or speech may be different. These people may be foreigners to a culture, they may be physically disabled or mentally impaired. Perhaps they are hard to understand, or they use a wheelchair, or their appearance is disfigured. This story is about the abuse these people suffer and how wrong it is to mistreat them.

Certainly there is a lesson in this story for children and for parents who fail to train and educate their children how to respect people who are different. Empathy is a maturity factor that increases with the development of certain regions in the brain. That is why children tend to be blunt and unfeeling. They are too young to put themselves in the shoes of the sufferer. Therefore, an important part of child rearing is teaching children that people who are different are *special* and that it is a privilege to care for a special person. They also need to understand the emotional pain people experience when they are treated poorly.

My wife, Barbara, began her career as a physical therapist in a clinic for disabled children. Their disabilities ranged from outpatients with Down syndrome to live-in care for severely retarded children. Barbara has no problem befriending people who are different, touching them, and chatting with them as easily as she would any of her coworkers. What these disabled children want from strangers is a smile. What they don't want is to be stared at—staring makes them feel uncomfortable.

When the children came out of the town and jeered at Elisha, they erased his value as a person. His role as a prophet and man of God was lost, hidden behind an unusual physical feature. As a person, his dignity was also erased. The abuse dished out by these children is the same type that makes people today feel isolated and worthless.

The fact that Elisha "looked" at the youths before speaking makes me wonder if he paused to calculate his reaction. I wonder if he even took a moment to consult God. The terror that fell on the children came from God, even though Elisha's curse invoked it. God is ultimately the One who speaks through this story. Everyone who heard this story afterward would be struck by the severity of the punishment. Whether the children were severely injured or killed, whether they were themselves disfigured for a time or for life, the point of the story is to convey the serious nature of mistreating people who are different. The story illustrates vividly the command of God, "Do not curse the deaf or put a stumbling block in front of the blind, but fear your God. I am the LORD" (Leviticus 19:14).

I have indulged in a little preaching while exploring our reactions to this passage—at any rate, preaching *is* my day job. Since I have already stepped out there, I will venture another remark or two.

Some people are embarrassed to sit next to a disabled person at a public event. Yes, those with a disability do draw the attention of others, and depending on their disability they may make a scene or need a little bit of help with simple tasks. But if you can forget yourself for a moment, it is rather easy to make another human being feel important. There are some people who rejoice for days afterward when they receive a simple hug. Whenever you lend them a hand, greet them as you would any other person, or defend them from abuse, you are walking in the footsteps of the saints—though, truth to tell, every Christian is called to sainthood.

> Then the righteous will answer him, "Lord, when did we see you hungry and feed you, or thirsty and give you something to drink? When did we see you a stranger and invite you in, or needing clothes and clothe you? When did we see you sick or in prison and go to visit you?"
>
> The King will reply, "I tell you the truth, whatever you did for one of the least of these brothers of mine, you did for me."
> (Matthew 25:37-40)

Did you read the above passage? If not, go back and read it. If you read it already, try reading it again. And as you read, think carefully about what the text does, how it affects you, what it makes you feel. Make the Word of God personal by paying careful attention to what it does within you. Let the Word of God "dwell in you richly" (Colossians 3:16) and speak to your soul. Find out what the text *does* in your life, then act on it.

CHAPTER 6

WHAT DOES THE TEXT SAY — AND HOW?

Paying Attention to the Formal Details

I have in front of me a photograph of my daughter, Karen, standing next to a young man by the stairway in our house. They are smiling nervously. Now I should tell you, Karen is very lovely even when she goes grubby in faded blue jeans. But in this picture, she is especially radiant because she is dressed for her school's winter formal.

A winter formal, as the name implies, involves formal attire, formal dining, and formal activities. The word *formal,* however, merely describes the superficial aspects of the evening. It fails to describe the interactions between the students—the substance of their conversations and the slang they use.

If a winter formal can be fully defined by its surface features, then the real life of the students who participate in it is irrelevant. They could just as well be paid models in formalwear standing in for actual high schoolers. The word *formal* denotes only the outer shell of this event. When high school students get dressed up, it is to play a role. They are still normal, *informal* teenagers on the inside.

WHAT'S WINTER IN A RAIN FOREST?

Suppose you lived in a culture that knew nothing of winter formals, but you heard about this strange custom and thought it would make for an interesting study. All you had available to you was ten or twenty still photos taken at a formal event. You would have to carefully examine the pictures and draw conclusions. After taking your first pass through the photos you might say, "I have found an underlying unity: These people are all wearing formal attire."

To learn anything more about the winter formal phenomenon you would try to figure out how every detail in the photos related to the whole event. You might notice an age difference between students and teachers. You might look closely at the tables, place settings, and centerpieces. You may notice that the same person appears in several photographs, engaged in a variety of activities (conversing, dancing, eating, making faces). Perhaps you're able to learn something about the musical entertainment. But still, you have only scratched the surface, and to improve your research, you'll have to pay even closer attention to even the most minute details.

Through careful reasoning and a smattering of imagination, you would learn a great deal about winter formals. Of course, imagination could get you into trouble, but without it you could never explore the potential relationships between the details you observe. When you ask, "What is the meaning of that gesture or that item of apparel?" you must be able to imagine a use for such things and how they relate to the "formalness" of all the other details.

This type of research is similar to an interpretive tool that we'll refer to as *paying attention to the details.* All we know about the writers and characters of the Bible is found in the pictures we find in the text. From this, we can't learn much about their personal psychology, daily frustrations, travel experiences, and so on. In his letters, Paul mentioned different types of people: the good guys (Andronicus and Junias), the bad guys (Hymenaeus and Alexander), and the bad guys who became good guys—

or vice versa—such as Demas. But most of these people we know only from Paul's perspective through his writing.

Paying attention to the details means that we look closely, not only at the substance of the text, but also at what appears on the surface—its *shell.* We pay attention to the words, sentence structure, plot twists, images, and other features to discover how a story or description interrelates. We begin with the assumptions that there is a unity within the passage and it can be discovered through careful examination. Once we see the unity, we pick our way through each verse to find how every little shift, repetition, and nuance relates to the unifying theme.

THE BIG IDEA:

If we pay attention to the details—form, patterns, cadence, word usage, and other devices—an underlying unity will emerge that reveals an interrelatedness of all its parts, and another level of meaning is revealed.

A DETAILED EXAMPLE

Let's try an exercise in paying attention to the details. In John 13, Jesus surprised His disciples by washing their feet. When He had finished making the rounds, He explained why He took on this humiliating chore. Throughout the passage we find the theme of love, which Jesus eventually turned into a command in verse 34. But the love was of a specific nature; it was His own love that He wanted to plant in their hearts, "As I have loved you, so you must love one another" (13:34). The foot washing was a living demonstration of the kind of service people perform for those they love. The unifying theme of the passage is love in action, a kind of love that becomes visible in its expression of service.

When we look at the details, many things draw our attention. Here is just one. After Jesus gave the disciples a living example of love, and after explaining the meaning of His actions, He capped His teaching with the words, "Now that you know these things, you will be blessed if you do them" (13:17). Notice that *knowing* "these things" is not enough, the disciples must *do* them. The love that Jesus wants the disciples to adopt is not a way of feeling or thinking, but a way of acting.

When we look carefully at the way John tells the story, we discover that he reinforced Jesus' teaching in telling us about His personal example. John built a subtle message into the structure of the story. Look at verses 4 and 5:

So he [Jesus] got up from the meal, took off his outer clothing, and wrapped a towel around his waist. After that, he poured water into a basin and began to wash his disciples' feet, drying them with the towel that was wrapped around him.

There is a lot of action in these two verses. In fact, the *New International Version* even combines two verbs that appear separately in the Greek text: Jesus took a towel, then "girded Himself" (NASB). Thus, seven actions are condensed into two verses and one smooth movement as Jesus went from His place at the table to kneeling at the feet of the first disciple.

Why does John load this story with so many verbs when he could simply say, "Jesus began washing the disciples' feet"? Perhaps John wants to stress the active nature of love. So he begins the story by establishing the unifying theme, telling us that Jesus "loved his own who were in the world" (13:1). Then he immediately shows us how that love behaved. A few moments later Jesus explained, "Now that you know these things, you will be blessed if you do them" (13:17).

Up front, John tells us that Jesus *knew* some things. During the course of the evening it becomes obvious that Jesus wanted His disciples to know some things too. In His creative style of teaching, Jesus taught first by presenting a living picture, then by explanation. At first the disciples didn't know what Jesus had done to them (see 13:7,12), but afterward they knew. Still, knowing was not enough. The blessing was not in knowing, but in doing.

WATCH YOUR STEP

As we use the interpretive tool of paying attention to the details, we need to be aware of its risks. The people who did the most intensive work in this method of literary interpretation belonged to the schools of Russian Formalism and, in its wake, the New Criticism. These scholars argued that once a text was written and made public, it no longer belonged to the author. A word, when *spoken,* can't be separated from the speaker, because he has to be present in order for the word to be uttered. In contrast, a written word does not require the presence of the author and continues to exist long after the author has died. Therefore, the formalists concluded that it is a mistake (or fallacy) to ask about the author's intention when looking for the meaning of a written text. The meaning is *in* the text itself and not in the mind of the author, which we can never know. The text was thought to be a self-contained entity in which every clue was found and every question answered within its own circumference, without regard to the author's intent.

Those who argue that the Bible must be studied strictly as literature, and not as God's revelation to us, usually have a formalist approach in mind. They would sever the Bible from the basic communication model of writer-text-reader and examine it as an isolated piece of art. But if we disconnect the Bible from God's authorship, it is nothing more than a human creation. And if we disregard the intended effect on the reader, to open his or her eyes to God's truth, then we rob God's Word of its meaning. We can never separate the text from the God who inspired it and the readers who study it.

A second risk we take when we pay strict attention to the details is losing sight of the forest for the trees. We can become so intent on finding the hidden clues that we overread the text and exaggerate one element's relationship to another. We can become too clever in the way we create links between the details and the text's central theme. Paying attention to the details runs the risk of demonstrating the ingenuity of the interpreter rather than the beauty and meaning of the text.

The details, while incredibly enlightening, must always be interpreted in light of the text's intended message. Isolating the formal aspects of a text can lead to the sad result of finding a code without a message—details of the text without a clue to God's intent. Imagine yourself in the mountains on a dark night. From a mountainside across a lake you see a series of flashes. You realize there are long and short bursts of light. Perhaps someone is sending a message in Morse code. You whip out your Boy Scout handbook and begin deciphering the code. Soon you discover that the person on the opposite shore is not sending a message but merely flashing random letters, perhaps practicing the code. Studying what you thought was a meaningful code failed to produce a message.

The writers of the Bible were not flashing meaningless signals as they wrote under God's inspiration. So when we interpret Scripture, we must first find and heed the message rather than getting lost in the details. The heart of what God has to say is in the message. The code is merely a device for enhancing, illustrating, or emphasizing the message.

In the first chapter of this book we saw that one way to avoid overinterpreting a passage is to stay close to its literal meaning.[1] The historical and grammatical interpretation of a passage must always come first, and the meaning we find there limits the scope of all other interpretations. No matter what we think the details tell us, any meaning that goes beyond what has been established by rational exegesis should be regarded with great skepticism.

GETTING THE MOST FROM FORMAL DETAILS

To gain the maximum benefit from the careful study of formal details, we need to acquire three basic skills: observation, meditation, and recording. Fortunately, these skills develop rapidly with a little practice.

OBSERVATION

If you rush the process, you'll never uncover deeper levels of meaning in the Bible. It takes time to become observant. In developing this skill, the force of habit and your familiarity with Scripture can work against you. We constantly do the familiar things in life without even thinking about them. We get dressed every morning while our minds are engaged in myriad other thoughts. We can take the regular route to work five days a week without ever noticing the details of what is happening along the way. The same lack of awareness can occur when we return to a familiar passage of Scripture.

To become observant, we learn to focus our concentration on specific points of interest. You can pick up the items on your grocery list without once looking in the eyes of another shopper or being aware that the store's sound system is playing an old Beatles song. As you go about your day, you filter out much more sensory stimuli than you are aware of. So stop for a moment, close your eyes, and be still. How many different sounds do you hear and what is producing them? Is there a dominant odor in your environment? What is the temperature? Is there any movement of air? What is the texture of your environment? How do your clothes feel against your skin—soft, stiff, scratchy? These stimuli are constantly present, but you don't become fully conscious of your surroundings until you stop and focus your attention.

In a similar way we can become conscious of what is in a passage of Scripture once we train our focus on particular themes and details. Suddenly a word, an action, a rhythm jumps from the page. We discover a thread of thought, and following it leads to an image or wordplay that reinforces that theme. We begin to see things we never knew were there.

When we are paying attention to the details, everything we are looking for is already in the text. Therefore, we sit in front of a passage and stare at it as if it were an elaborate painting and our job is to become well acquainted with its every feature.

MEDITATION

Observation alone will not break open the meaning of a passage. We need to contemplate the whole passage and meditate on its individual parts. Sometimes you will read a passage and not find its unifying theme. Other times the theme will come easily but seem too insignificant. In that instance, saturate your mind with the passage by reading it again and again. Remind yourself that there is a deep theme or message in the passage, and then live with the passage for a while. Observing details and then meditating on a passage takes us into its heart, and the particulars we discover stick in our minds—not necessarily verbatim, but in our own understanding of the text.

RECORDING

Rounding out the skill of observation is the practice of recording—jotting down a few notes or drawing a diagram or graph based on the text. It is often useful to make an outline or draw a tree graph (a central box with lines that branch out from it, usually with the theme written in the box and the particulars written on the lines). Using the tree-graph approach has the advantage of keeping our attention on the central theme and demonstrating how all the details relate to it.

Making a record of our thoughts not only helps us remember what we have discovered, but the exercise of writing engages a part of our brain not used in reading and helps us to see even more than we saw before. And if God has spoken to us, it's always a good idea to preserve what He has said.

WHAT TO LOOK FOR

Searching through the text's formal elements means we are looking for just about everything. But a great place to begin is to read an entire book of the Bible all the way through. We are interested in the themes that will emerge, although they may not be easy to find. Often, the first theme we think we discover will be replaced by another as we move into a more careful reading. When we pay attention to the text, it is important to avoid cross-references to any other book in the Bible. If something in the text confuses you, make a note of it, but don't attempt to resolve it immediately.

As you read the entire book, look for irony, paradox, and any tensions or conflicts that occur. For example, in the book of Job there is an ongoing tension between Job and his friends. Job's suffering pushes him outside the simplistic worldview that good people get good things in life and bad people get trouble and sorrow. His friends use all sorts of strategies to break Job but without success. Knowing the tension in the text helps us to discern their misguided tactics.

Since some books of the Bible are too lengthy for such a close reading, you will need to break down the text passage by passage. To help determine where the passage begins and ends, remember that it will always be one complete unit of thought. As you examine the passage, look for the following:

- The overall "shape" of the text. Look for patterns, repetition, shifts in thought, the mood that builds, and the narrator's point of view. Several of the psalms were written as acrostics (the first letter of each verse begins with a letter of the Hebrew alphabet, like "A is for apple, B is for ball"), the most notable being Psalm 119.
- The passage's main theme. Follow the theme, and determine its climax and how it is achieved. Then review the passage and discover how its separate parts relate to the main theme.
- The individual ideas. Is there anything disturbing, unusual, or seemingly out of place? How do the ideas fit together?
- In poetry, look for paradox, poetic devices, and rhythm. (Some Bible commentaries are helpful in illuminating Hebrew poetry.) In history and narrative (stories), look for plot and character development.
- The sound of the text (reading aloud will help). Do you hear a rhythm or cadence? Listen for specific sounds; for instance,

alliteration. Of course, there is more of this type of device in the original language than in English translations. Listen also for the tone of voice in the passage.

- The words themselves. Are there any strange words, or are any words used in a strange way? Do any of them have double meanings?
- The interrelations of the various parts to the whole. For instance, is a word used symbolically to represent something else in the text? How is the theme represented in the structure of the passage? How is the theme supported by metaphors or figures of speech?
- Unusual applications of different elements. For instance, could there be a symbolic use of location, a plant that is mentioned, or a particular object?

As you analyze the formal details of a text, discuss your discoveries with other people, preferably a group of people who share the same interest, and if possible, a Bible scholar (who may be a pastor in your church).

WHO SAID WHAT

As you read the passage, pay special attention to the point of view. Within every text there is a narrator who is doing the speaking. Point of view has to do with the narrator's relationship to the text. Sometimes the text is written in the first person, in which case the narrator uses the personal pronouns *I, me, my.* In the book of Acts, the narrator sometimes writes in the third person (for instance, "When *they* arrived in Salamis, *they* proclaimed the word of God" [Acts 13:5]) and sometimes in the first-person plural ("When *we* arrived at Jerusalem, the brothers received *us* warmly" [Acts 21:17]).

Sometimes the narrator hovers over the passage as if he were all-knowing. Thus everything in the story is known to the narrator. The narrator of the book of Job was aware of a conversation in heaven between God and Satan, a circumstance that was unknown to Job and his friends.

Sometimes the narrator has a limited point of view, as when the psalmist is depressed and unable to see the outcome of his circumstances (see, for example, Psalm 142).

There is one point of view that never occurs in the Bible: a detached, "scientific" point of view. For hundreds of years, to "do science" meant to stand back from a subject and study it as if completely detached from it. It was believed that emotional involvement corrupted objectivity and tainted pure research. However, we never see this approach in Scripture. In every part of the Bible, the narrator is connected to the story, issues, people, or information in the text. Therefore the narrator will always stand somewhere, and one of your challenges will be to determine just where he stands. Is the narrator in sympathy with the characters or opposed to them? Does the narrator have beliefs or values that come to light in the way the story is told? Is the narrator concerned with the outcome of the story?

CASE STUDY: THE BOOK OF ECCLESIASTES

Let's put this new interpretive method to work in the book of Ecclesiastes. For a fair demonstration, we'll take no more than the first fifteen verses of the first chapter.

The words of the Teacher, son of David, king in Jerusalem:

"Meaningless! Meaningless!"
    says the Teacher.
"Utterly meaningless!
    Everything is meaningless!"

What does man gain from all his labor
    at which he toils under the sun?
Generations come and generations go,
    but the earth remains forever.

The sun rises and the sun sets,
  and hurries back to where it rises.
The wind blows to the south
  and turns to the north
round and round it goes,
  ever returning on its course.
All streams flow into the sea,
  yet the sea is never full.
To the place the streams come from,
  there they return again.
All things are wearisome,
  more than one can say.
The eye never has enough of seeing,
  nor the ear its fill of hearing.
What has been will be again,
  what has been done will be done again;
  there is nothing new under the sun.
Is there anything of which one can say,
  "Look! This is something new"?
It was here already, long ago;
  it was here before our time.
There is no remembrance of men of old,
  and even those who are yet to come
will not be remembered
  by those who follow.

I, the Teacher, was king of Israel in Jerusalem. I devoted myself to study and to explore by wisdom all that is done under heaven. What a heavy burden God has laid on men! I have seen all the things that are done under the sun; all of them are meaningless, a chasing after the wind.

What is twisted cannot be straightened;

what is lacking cannot be counted. (Ecclesiastes 1:1-15)

THE THEME

The narrator's first words give us a big clue in finding the central theme: "Meaningless! Meaningless!" says the Teacher. "Utterly meaningless! Everything is meaningless!" The number of times the word "meaningless" appears, almost to the point of redundancy, confirms our suspicion regarding the theme of this book. The English word "meaningless" translates the Hebrew word *hebel,* a term denoting emptiness and futility.

In Ecclesiastes, the narrator explores a broad range of human endeavors, only to draw the conclusion that every activity, even life itself, is absurd. As we prepare for a close reading of the text we'll want to see how the theme of absurdity is developed. But we will also discover a specific context in which the narrator's search for meaning takes place, and that is indicated by another oft-repeated phrase, "under the sun."

The phrase "under the sun" suggests a materialistic perspective of life. This is not life "before God," which in the Old Testament suggests an awareness of life's spiritual dimension. Rather, life "under the sun" lacks a consciousness of the transcendent reality beyond earthly existence. It is this naturalistic quest for meaning that results in absurdity.

God is not left out of Ecclesiastes, but when we look for Him we make an interesting discovery: The personal name of God, *Yahweh,* is never used. In the book of Ecclesiastes, we find the Hebrew word *Elohim,* or "God," which is not a name but a title. Elohim is used in the Old Testament in reference to God as Creator or Judge of all the nations and is less personal, more formal than Yahweh. It's similar to talking about a powerful official and using his formal title (Mr. President) rather than making it personal by using his given name (George).

Much of God's activity in Ecclesiastes is depicted as if it were a mechanical part of the infrastructure of the universe. Just as the sun's rising and setting can be viewed as a mechanical operation in the natural world, so God's rewarding good deeds and punishing wickedness can be seen as a mechanical operation in the moral sphere. God appears as the guardian of cause-and-effect relationships, and is, in fact, the ultimate Cause. He is, in this sense, even responsible for laying this "heavy burden" of meaninglessness on humans by bringing them into this absurd world (see Ecclesiastes 1:13-14).

POINT OF VIEW

Where does the narrator stand in relationship to the text? The first verse of the first chapter gives us our answer, "The words of the Teacher, son of David, king in Jerusalem." Bible commentators often refer to the narrator by his Hebrew title, *Qoheleth,* the Teacher (or Preacher), which means one who summons or addresses an assembly. Therefore, Ecclesiastes is a series of lectures or sermons delivered in the first person by the Teacher.

The narrator also describes himself as a descendant ("son") of David and king in Jerusalem. Since we are, at this point, concerned only with the formal aspects of the text, we do not need to determine which king this might be or if it was a scribe writing under the auspices of a king. Let's go with tradition and assign this work to Solomon, the only one of David's descendants who ruled over "Israel" from Jerusalem for any length of time. But what is more interesting to this method of interpretation is the fact that the narrator nowhere identifies himself by name. Instead, he uses the title "I, the Teacher" (1:12). We will respect the narrator's decision to remain the anonymous Teacher.

The other two pieces of information we have regarding the narrator demonstrate his credentials, letting us know he is qualified to go on this quest for meaning and has all the resources at his disposal to do it right. Thus the tone of voice is typical for the Wisdom Literature in which the reader is expected to adopt the role of a student and learn from the wise man.

However, we also want to take into consideration that the Teacher is a jaded intellectual. Several times he tells us there is nothing better for humans than to enjoy their meaningless lives as best they can (see 5:18). If the Teacher lived in the twentieth century, he likely would have been a cynical existentialist.

MAKING CONNECTIONS

Now that we've identified the theme and the narrator's point of view, we'll look for connections between the theme and the particulars and for the interplay of words, symbols, and ideas. We may want to interrogate some of the images that occur. For instance, we might ask, What else could this (person, place, thing) stand for other than the literal object that it represents? What sort of concept could it symbolize? We also will pay close attention to figures of speech, especially if they are repeated.

Stepping into the text we bump into the question, "What does man gain from all his labor at which he toils under the sun?" (1:3). "Toil" appears to be the nature of life "under the sun," and the Teacher tells us there is no "gain" from it. This theme will reappear. The Teacher will ask what people get, gain, or profit from all of their work and investments, and he will conclude that it's all meaningless.

STRUCTURE AND METAPHORS

The next movement in the passage is loaded with interesting allusions. First, there are four big cycles: generations coming and going; the sun rising and setting; the wind blowing "round and round"; and streams flowing to sea, evaporating, and returning to their origin, yet they accomplish nothing because "the sea is never full." In other words, everything is going in circles. There is no progress. The rising and setting sun may give us the illusion of a new day, but today is really a repetition of yesterday. This concept is reiterated in verses 9 and 10:

> What has been will be again,
>> what has been done will be done again;
>> there is nothing new under the sun.

Is there anything of which one can say,
"Look! This is something new"?
It was here already, long ago;
it was here before our time.

You may think you have a new idea, but someone else had the same idea long ago.

This dreary idea of being stuck in an endless, unbreakable cycle is reminiscent of the Greek myth of Sisyphus. Because he displeased Zeus, his punishment in Hades was to push a rock up a hill. Every time he almost reached the summit, the rock would roll all the way back down, and Sisyphus would have to begin again—for all eternity. The repetition of the same activity every day was perceived to be a punishment of the gods. For the Teacher, this meaningless repetition is what constitutes the absurdity of life. Humans are trapped on this huge merry-go-round, as "generations come and generations go, but the earth remains forever" (1:4).

A second thought emerges: "Earth," "sun," "wind," and "sea" represent the building blocks of nature. This parallels the thinking of the early Greek philosophers who identified the basic elements of the universe as earth, fire, air, and water. If even the fundamental forces or substances of the universe are caught in these endless cycles, then the absurd nature of life "under the sun" is not just our imagination. We are victims of the same meaningless repetition that brings the sun, wind, and sea back to their starting points only to begin their circular course again. Absurdity is woven into the fabric of nature itself.

The Teacher's reference to the sun reminds us that his investigation was "under the sun." The sun is powerful as a source of light and heat, but it has no power to transform. The sun merely helps to illumine the absurdity of life (see 6:1). Also, ancient civilizations had this image of the sun descending below the horizon, fighting a horrific battle with the dark underworld, then reemerging to run across the sky again. So after it sets, it "hurries back to where it rises." The Hebrew word translated "hurries" is *sho-ap* and means to gasp for breath or pant. Here is a picture of a worn-out runner racing through the night, only to rise and set once again.

Another fascinating concept in this list of cyclical mechanisms of nature is the wind. The wind is a kind of nothingness. The Hebrew word for wind, *ruach,* is capable of several meanings: wind, breath, spirit, even intense emotion. The only way to know how to translate *ruach* is by its context. The words that surround it determine whether we are talking about breath, wind, or spirit. (For an interesting study, compare the way the *King James Version* tends to translate *ruach* as "spirit" in Ecclesiastes and the *New International Version*'s tendency to translate it as "wind.")

In a later chapter of Ecclesiastes, the Teacher will ask, "Who knows if the spirit *[ruach]* of man rises upward and if the spirit of the animal goes down into the earth?" (3:21). The spirit, like the wind, is an insubstantial and unknowable entity. And "all the things that are done under the sun" are no more than "a chasing after the wind" (1:14,17). To chase the wind—which is another recurring phrase—is an absurd quest. It is the pursuit of nothingness.

The place of humans in all of this cyclical nonsense is generalized by the Teacher. In other words, he does not say, "Our ancestors came and went, we are here and will go, our descendants will come and go," but "Generations come and go." In verse 8 he does not say, "Our eyes never see enough," or "Your eyes…," or "My eyes…," but simply, "The eye…" That is because one human life cannot be distinguished from another, except that some are wicked and some are righteous, some are poor and some are rich, some are wise and some are foolish, but it doesn't matter because "the same fate overtakes them both" (2:14-16). In fact, in this regard humans are no better off than animals, "the same fate awaits them both: As one dies, so dies the other" (3:19).

THE SOUND OF THE TEXT

Let's take one more pass through these verses to listen to how they *sound*. You might want to read the quotation out loud so you can listen to its rhythm. I quote from the *King James Version* because of its literary quality:

> One generation passeth away, and another generation cometh: but the earth abideth forever. The sun also ariseth, and the sun goeth down, and hasteth to his place where he arose. The wind goeth toward the south, and turneth about unto the north; it whirleth about continually, and the wind returneth again according to his circuits. All the rivers run into the sea; yet the sea is not full; unto the place from whence the rivers come, thither they return again. (1:4-7)

Did you notice the uneven cadence? If you try to make these verses march to a beat, you will find they resist simple rhythm. In fact, one way they refuse to be read rhythmically is by increasing the number of syllables in each successive verse. (In Hebrew, the text has something like sixteen syllables in verse 4, twenty-three in verse 5, twenty-eight in verse 6, and thirty-seven in verse 7.)

The harder you try to establish a cadence, the more frustrating it becomes. You cannot stretch each stanza and establish a consistent meter. By the time you get to verse 8 you are in full agreement with the Teacher that "all things are wearisome, more than one can say." That is exactly your experience with the *structure* of the text. The Teacher's lesson is illustrated in the uneven pattern of the words.

THE WORDS OF THE TEXT

If we take another look at the "eye" and the "ear" (1:8), we discover that they never get their fill. So no matter how many years we live, no matter how much we see and hear, no matter how much effort we pour into life, we never reach a point of satisfaction. We are running in place on the hamster's wheel, and no matter what we do, we're destined to die wishing we had seen and heard more. To be sure, "all things are wearisome, more than one can say" (1:8).

In Romans 8, Paul wrote that "the creation was subjected to frustration, not by its own choice, but by the will of the one who subjected it, in hope that the creation itself will be liberated from its bondage to decay and brought into the glorious freedom of the children of God" (8:20-21). The Greek word that the *New International Version* translates as "frustration" in Romans 8 is the same word translated as "meaningless" from the Greek translation of Ecclesiastes. Paul *tells* us that creation, of which we are a part, is "subjected to frustration," or meaninglessness. The writer of Ecclesiastes, however, makes us *feel* that frustration.

The value of the poetic form of Ecclesiastes is that it leads us to an experience. We may see people who are wealthy, hedonistic, or extremely successful and think, *Wow, what a great life they lead!* But Ecclesiastes enables us to feel the emptiness and futility of any life apart from God. We do not simply *learn* that life "under the sun" is meaningless, we *experience* that wearisome futility in the cyclical language of the Teacher.

CONCLUSION

Earlier I made the point that one of the exercises of this interpretive method is to discuss your discoveries with other people and, if possible, talk it over with a biblical scholar. To get the most out of this method of interpretation requires dialogue with others who are willing to pass around their own ideas, discuss and critique them together, then return to the text for more discoveries. If you invest in this worthwhile pursuit, you'll be spending quality time with the Bible and with others who share your spiritual hunger. When you apply this method to your favorite passages of Scripture, you will be amazed as you find that there is so much more in God's Word than you've ever seen before.

CHAPTER 7

MUCH ABOUT HISTORY

Paying Attention to the
Historical Backdrop

Have you ever rummaged through a box of old letters that belonged to someone else? I know of a man who has dozens of picture postcards that were sent to Missouri addresses in the early 1900s. Each card bears a vague rural address, the first and last name of the recipient, and a postmark from a nearby town.

Beyond those few specifics, however, the messages written on the cards raise all sorts of questions. Most of them are signed only with the writer's first name. Was this person a relative, a friend, a work associate? References to other people identified only by a first name leave us to wonder if they were mutual acquaintances, distant relatives, or immediate family. One postcard writer needed to be picked up on a certain date at a train station but failed to specify which station. Of course, the family that received the card ninety years ago knew where to pick up their visitor, but we would have to do some serious detective work today to locate the right depot.

These old postcards illustrate just a few of the difficulties we encounter when we read a text apart from its historical context. Even though many of the postcards were sent to the same person over a period of only a few years, the written messages still leave big holes in our understanding. When trying to interpret them, we discover our ignorance regarding the background against which they were written.

Interpreting the postcards poses an identical challenge to our attempts to interpret the New Testament epistles. So we must ask: Is there a way to *get behind* the text for a better understanding of its message? "Word studies" and language alone will not help us. Without knowing the context of the New Testament epistles, there will always be missing pieces of information that obscure the message. The more knowledge a writer and reader share in common, the fewer facts they need to provide. If we do not have access to that common knowledge, then we must dig outside and behind the text to learn all we can. The text is consistently illumined by context.

Our study of New Testament letters is greatly enhanced when we shine the light of historical context on them. The same is true with every book in the Bible, seeing that they were written in the ancient Near East—a context that could hardly be more foreign to contemporary North America.

Every writer, biblical or otherwise, assumes shared knowledge, information, or experience with his readers. Writer and reader have to share at least a small pool of knowledge to understand what the other means.

THE BIG IDEA:

The historical background of a biblical passage provides important clues to its meaning. In fact, some details can be understood *only* in their historical context.

"PLEASE STAY ON THE TRAIL"

Like other methods of interpretation, paying attention to historical background presents certain perils if we wander from the trail. Some Bible teachers become so engrossed in showing us the Scriptures' ancient context that they never get around to connecting it to the present. I've heard people say that their preacher takes them into the past and leaves them there. If our goal is a godly lifestyle, we can't allow the study of history to become an obsession. We borrow and learn from history, but we need to do so without trying to return to the past or recreate it.

Another notion we want to avoid is that historical situations or events *produced* the biblical text. Some people treat the New Testament as if it were the natural consequence of cultural, political, and religious influences.[1] In recent history, the pendulum has swung to the opposite extreme among scholars who claim that the text is disconnected from its original circumstances, that its historical context is irrelevant. Between these extremes lies a middle ground in which the text is shaped, but not controlled, by its occurrence in time and space.

The dynamic nature of the sacred text prevents it from belonging to just one period of time. Isaiah used grass as a metaphor to describe the transience of human life compared to the eternal Word of God: "The grass withers and the flowers fall, but the word of our God stands forever" (Isaiah 40:8). Jesus made a similar statement regarding His own teaching: "Heaven and earth will pass away, but my words will never pass away" (Matthew 24:35). God's Word will continue to speak for as long as the universe exists.

SITES OF HISTORICAL SIGNIFICANCE

When we study a text's historical setting, we want to research archaeology, anthropology, ancient writings, and historiography. We want to learn about the geography, including cities and villages where events occurred. The development of ancient empires as well as their religions and social customs are of special interest. We want to learn about the political climate, the cultural conditions, and economics. We want to know the beliefs and worldview of the characters involved. We study their lifestyles, work, family life, and modes of travel. Even the weather typical of those regions will add depth to our understanding. If we can see, hear, and feel what the author experienced, look at the world as he did, and think his thoughts, we will find meanings that we would miss if we read the Bible only in our own context.

The New Testament was written against the background of the Roman Empire. The spiritual, cultural, and cognitive background was influenced by Judaism and Hellenistic philosophy. The abundant information available on the history of the Roman Empire, Greek philosophy, and Judaism will provide us with a good deal of useful information.[2]

Translators have made great strides in giving us the sense of the original languages, but there are some words, idioms, figures of speech, and grammatical constructions that simply do not translate. So when you study the historical background, keep your interpretations open. If new information is uncovered that proves former interpretations to be wrong or only partially correct, be ready to revise your position.

GATHERING HISTORICAL INFORMATION

Many times the content of a passage will dictate what kind of historical background we need to investigate. We acknowledge that the text was written in a particular *situation,* that it was meant to address a *situation,* and that the original readers also read the text within a given *situation.* The study of context moves through concentric circles, starting with the context immediately surrounding the text, then moving outward to take in the whole book, section of Scripture, and so on. In studying the historical background, we hope to find information regarding the following subjects:

The author. Is a biography of the author available either in the Bible or in reference works? Where was the book written (while the author was traveling, in exile, or in prison? what place or city or nation?), and what were the circumstances in that place? What are the author's credentials? Why did he, rather than someone else, write this book? There are books of the Bible whose author is unknown to us, but if we can at least locate the author in a specific era or school of thought, we will have a significant foothold for our interpretation.

The audience. To whom was this letter, book, or history written?

What were the circumstances of the intended audience? Were they masters, slaves, free citizens, or a mix? Were they farmers, soldiers, or merchants? What sort of education did they have? What was their worldview? What was their religious life like? What was their relationship to the author? Did they live in the heart of great civilizations, or were they rustic village folk?

The general environment. We want to know about the setting of the text, the author, and the initial readers. What do we know about the city of Jerusalem in the sixth century B.C.? What about Babylon in the fifth century B.C.? What can we learn about Corinth during the period of Paul's ministry there? What were the big cities like during the days of Abraham, and what was his own encampment like? What materials were used in constructing houses and public buildings, and how were they built? What were the religious beliefs and practices of the people?

The language. Certain words or phrases may be critical to the meaning of a passage. In such cases, we may need to research the background of those phrases to see how they were commonly used. Sometimes the use of specific terms is illumined by other biblical references.

The culture and customs. Communication is greatly influenced by culture. The values and worldview of a culture will influence what a writer feels is important to include or omit. Culture and local customs give shape to simple references that may be unknown in our day. What can we learn about the art, values, and daily practices of the writer's culture?

Politics and economics. What form of government prevailed in the environment of the writer and readers? Were they free citizens, subjects of a king, slaves of a pharaoh, living exiled in a foreign country, or living in their own country under foreign rule? How was political authority exercised? What was their form of currency, and how was it controlled—used in bartering or distributed through society?

Religions. What did the biblical writers have in mind when they talked about the gods of other nations or when talking about their own religious practices? What was their concept of God, angels, spirits, and life after death? What did they believe about the world of the supernatural—shamans or witches or prophets or seers? What do we know about the theology of the biblical writers?

Secular history. There is a lot we can learn about the life and times of biblical characters from historical records and other extrabiblical sources. Books on ancient world history, archaeology, and historians of the past can fill in a lot of details.

Since most of us are not trained historians, we have to be careful when we search for information. If we play fast and loose with the historical data, we will muddy rather than clarify the meaning of a passage. Consult Bible commentaries, dictionaries, encyclopedias, and almanacs to help direct and verify your research. If possible, interview (in person or by phone or e-mail) a professor of biblical history to keep your study on the right track.

CASE STUDY: PAUL'S FIRST LETTER TO TIMOTHY

Perhaps I should begin with the disclaimer "Don't try this at home." I have chosen a passage of Scripture that was the center of feverish study in the 1980s and 1990s and still remains a source of controversy. However, this passage is useful because of the volumes of historical data that have been unearthed around it, and it demonstrates how the meaning of a text in "plain English" can be a misleading notion for interpretation.[3] Further, I'm not suggesting that what follows is the final interpretation, but it highlights the way historical context can add depth to our understanding.[4]

Ready? Here's the passage:

> I want men everywhere to lift up holy hands in prayer, without anger or disputing.
>
> I also want women to dress modestly, with decency and propriety, not with braided hair or gold or pearls or expensive clothes,

but with good deeds, appropriate for women who profess to worship God.

A woman should learn in quietness and full submission. I do not permit a woman to teach or to have authority over a man; she must be silent. For Adam was formed first, then Eve. And Adam was not the one deceived; it was the woman who was deceived and became a sinner. But women will be saved through childbearing—if they continue in faith, love and holiness with propriety. (1 Timothy 2:8-15)

WHO AND TO WHOM?

The first sentence of 1 Timothy identifies "Paul, an apostle of Christ Jesus" as the writer (1:1). We know that Paul was bicultural (he belonged to both Hebrew and Roman worlds), he was a world traveler, and he was an important apostle. We will also do well to remember that Paul was not a woman-hater as some have charged. Given the male hegemony of his time, Paul could almost be considered a reformer in that he included the participation of women in public worship, including prophecy and prayer (see 1 Corinthians 11:5). His policy was more inclusive than exclusive (see Galatians 3:28). However, he still had a deep concern for propriety and the reputation of the church within its cultural environment.

One other observation is that Paul had a traumatic experience in Ephesus (see Acts 19), a city and culture that provide essential background and context to Paul's letter to Timothy. We will take a close look at the Ephesus episode as part of our background research.

The letter is addressed to Timothy, which takes any guesswork out of identifying the original audience. Timothy was a young disciple who traveled with Paul. His mother was Jewish, but his father was Greek (see Acts 16:1). Timothy received spiritual and biblical instruction from his grandmother and mother "from infancy" (2 Timothy 1:5; 3:15). Scholars speculate that Timothy became a believer after Paul's first visit to Lystra and Derbe. Paul's affinity for Timothy is made clear in the way he addresses him as "my true son in the faith" and "my dear son" (1 Timothy 1:2; 2 Timothy 1:2).

Timothy was from Lystra (or perhaps nearby Derbe). The first time Paul visited Lystra, he and Barnabas were mistaken for the gods Zeus and Hermes (see Acts 14:12). This same city that was so ready to offer sacrifices to Paul later became hostile, stoning him and leaving him for dead (see Acts 14:19). Lystra was a small, rustic village that had been granted the status of a Roman colony. Given the Greek roots of Timothy's father and the fact of his marriage to a Jewish woman, it is likely that Timothy belonged to one of the well-to-do classes of Lystra's Roman population.

Timothy became a minister and was perhaps Paul's most devoted— and certainly Paul's most trusted—disciple (see Philippians 2:19-23). Paul and a group of elders had "laid their hands" on Timothy to set him aside for ministry and impart to him spiritual gifts (see 1 Timothy 4:14; 2 Timothy 1:6). Paul was apparently confident that Timothy could direct the affairs of several churches as his regional representative.

LOCATION, LOCATION, LOCATION

We can't say for certain where Paul was when he wrote this letter. But we know where Timothy was when he received the letter, and his location happens to be relevant to the interpretation of the 1 Timothy passage cited earlier:

> As I urged you when I went into Macedonia, stay there in Ephesus so that you may command certain men not to teach false doctrines any longer nor to devote themselves to myths and endless genealogies. These promote controversies rather than God's work—which is by faith. (1 Timothy 1:3-4)

We are not only told where Timothy was but why he was there and what Paul wanted him to do there.

Ephesus is prominent for at least three reasons: a significant event that we will examine in a moment, recorded in the book of Acts; the loveliness and theological depth of Paul's letter to the Ephesians; and the fact that it is one of the seven churches that received letters from Jesus in the book of Revelation. There is also a great deal of apostolic tradition that emanated from Ephesus, including stories of the apostle John's visits there, his disciple Polycarp, and the church fathers Irenaeus and Hypolytus. We also have a fair amount of information regarding Ephesus from secular history and archaeological discoveries.

According to Greek mythology, Ephesus was first settled by the Amazons. The word *Amazon* means "no breasts," because, as the story goes, these warrior women would remove one breast in order to be more proficient with weapons, such as the bow. Certainly goddess worship was well entrenched in the Ephesian culture long before the Greeks arrived. Ephesus enjoyed the prosperity and commerce of one of Asia's most important seaports. By the time of Paul's first visit to Ephesus, it was considered the religious center for the whole province of Asia because of the prestige of the goddess of Ephesus. Therefore it is not surprising that the result of Paul's teaching in the school of Tyrannus was that "all the Jews and Greeks who lived in the province of Asia heard the word of the Lord" (Acts 19:10).

Almost any encyclopedia article on Ephesus will feature the temple of Artemis—one of the seven wonders of the ancient world. For some reason, the translators of the *King James Version* refer to this Ephesian goddess as "Diana" (the name of the Roman goddess), but her Greek name, and that which is used in the biblical text, is Artemis.

There were actually two goddesses of Ephesian history that need to be distinguished. The earliest, Artemis Ephesia, was the most ancient goddess native to Anatolia. She was the "Mother goddess" of all living things. This ancient goddess was associated with the well-known statue of Artemis that was sheltered in her temple. One of her primary symbols is a bee that appears on many coins from Ephesus.

The other Artemis, the Greek goddess Artemis, was the daughter of

Zeus and Leto, and she was the twin sibling of Apollo. She was a hunter whose symbol was a bow with arrows. The Greek Artemis was associated with chastity and offered protection to virgins, but she also watched over mothers through childbirth. Eventually, the two goddesses merged into one cult, although the local population never relinquished the earlier beliefs that were attached to Artemis Ephesia.

The temple of Artemis was built, destroyed, and rebuilt several times. The temple was made of marble except for the tile roof, which was supported by more than one hundred pillars, each of which was sixty feet tall and decorated with Ionic capitals.

ARTEMIS OF THE EPHESIANS

We turn now to Acts 19 to dig up some background information. In chapter 18, Paul had passed through Ephesus, stopping long enough to introduce the gospel in the synagogue. He left Priscilla and Aquila in Ephesus when he traveled on to strengthen fledgling churches in other areas. Later Apollos arrived in Ephesus and taught about Jesus, although "he knew only the baptism of John" (see Acts 18:19-26). Priscilla and her husband invited Apollos to their home where they shared with him a more adequate explanation of the way of God.

When Paul returned to Ephesus, he encountered a group of disciples who also knew only the baptism of John and had not heard about the gift of the Holy Spirit. Paul taught them about Jesus and baptized them in His name. He then returned to the synagogue where he taught for about three months. When the Jews there refused to accept his message, Paul held discussions in a public lecture hall for two years.

Paul's stretch in Ephesus was accompanied by bizarre, supernatural phenomena. When seven exorcists combined the names of Jesus and Paul in an attempt to drive out an evil spirit, they were severely beaten by the possessed individual. Afterward, many of the Ephesians were moved to make a public confession of their deeds and renounce their former practice of sorcery. The value of the books they burned—50,000 pieces of silver—reveals to what degree sorcery and occultism flourished in Ephesus.

About the time that Paul made preparations to return to Jerusalem, a crisis occurred involving a silversmith named Demetrius (Acts 19:24). Demetrius and his colleagues made and sold small replicas of the shrine of Artemis. Archaeologists have recovered many of these shrines. The cheaper ones for the poor were made of terra cotta, whereas the more expensive ones were made of marble or silver. The shrines were offerings that devotees of Artemis presented to her in her temple.

The silversmiths made a healthy income from their trade, but they felt it was jeopardized by Paul's teaching. Demetrius warned his fellow artisans that not only their livelihood, but also the temple—and by implication, Artemis—were threatened. In saying this, Demetrius touched a deep nerve.

What happened next was something like a spontaneous strike of a powerful union, and all the tradesmen began to chant, "Great is Artemis of the Ephesians!" In a short while, "the whole city was in an uproar" and rushed two of Paul's traveling companions into the theater. This was probably the only structure that could accommodate the number of people who turned out to defend the goddess. For two hours the crowd shouted down the Christians and Jews with the chant, "Great is Artemis of the Ephesians!"

It is difficult for us to fathom their religious devotion. As the city clerk said, the whole world knew that Ephesus was the "guardian of the temple of the great Artemis and of her image, which fell from heaven" (Acts 19:35). To be a guardian (Greek, *neokoros*) was a great honor that many important cities were denied. It is possible that many Ephesians believed if they failed to defend the Artemisium—temple area of Artemis—she would severely punish them.

Paul experienced a good measure of success in his ministry to the Ephesians, but he also ran into significant obstacles (see 1 Corinthians 16:8-9). In fact, in some manner he "fought wild beasts in Ephesus" to the point that he nearly lost his life (see 1 Corinthians 15:30-32). Paul also realized that once he left Ephesus, the church there would be subject to teachers who would "distort the truth in order to draw away disciples after them" (Acts 20:29-30). So even though the church in Ephesus seemed to be strong and well supplied with spiritual leadership, Paul was still concerned that it might falter if the elders did not keep a careful watch.

THE CULT OF ARTEMIS

The more we learn about the Artemis cult, the more we will understand the words of Paul to Timothy. For example, Artemis insisted that all young people abstain from sex until marriage and then remain monogamous through life. Young women about to enter marriage would offer dolls and locks of their hair to Artemis, marking both the loss of their virginity and their complete devotion to the goddess. Married women were forbidden to enter the temple. Special offerings were also made by women who looked to the goddess for protection in childbirth.

There was an annual (or seasonal) procession in which the statue of Artemis was carried around the *via sacra* of Ephesus. The title "adorners of the goddess" is found in many inscriptions, and the women who served this role would be responsible to dress the goddess for her journey, which included stops at various shrines or monuments. The influence of Artemis was felt in every facet of the political and cultural climate of Ephesus and permeated the personal lives of its citizens.

MOVING THROUGH THE TEXT

Paul's instructions to Timothy are based on the premise that Timothy needed to know "how people ought to conduct themselves in God's household,...the pillar and foundation of the truth" (1 Timothy 3:15). Therefore he needed to know the criteria for appointing elders, deacons, and deacons' wives (or female deacons, see 3:11). Timothy also needed to know about care for widows and respect for leaders. But one of Paul's greatest concerns was the prevalence of false teaching that consisted of "myths," "endless genealogies," "old wives' tales," and "godless chatter" (1:4; 4:7; 6:20).

In the context of church life, Paul saw important roles for believers and specific roles for men and women. All members of the church were responsible to pray for every kind of earthly leader so Christians could lead "peaceful and quiet lives in all godliness and holiness." And if this prayer were answered, other people would be brought to a "knowledge of the truth" (2:1-4).

Within two sentences, Paul makes mention of the fact that God is our "Savior" and Jesus the *man* is our "mediator." These may be stabs at the Artemis cult. First, the devotees of Artemis called upon her as "Lord," "Savior," and "Queen of the Cosmos." Second, it was not the female goddess Artemis, but the *man* Christ Jesus who was the one mediator between God and humans (*anthropon,* generic for human being, either male or female).

From the men of the church, Paul wanted "holy hands" lifted in prayer (see verse 8). He did *not* want "anger or disputing" (verse 8). Paul's concern for holy hands may have been drawn from Psalm 24 where the poet outlined the prerequisites for "ascend[ing] the hill of the LORD" and standing in "his holy place" (Psalm 24:3)—an allusion to the worship of God in His temple. The person who qualifies "has clean hands and a pure heart, who does not lift up his soul to an idol or swear by what is false" (Psalm 24:4). If Paul did have this passage in mind, then the conditions for public prayer in the context of Ephesus are well defined. The man who did not have clean hands or who lifted his soul to an idol would be disqualified from worship in the presence of God.

From the women of the church, Paul wanted modest clothing and that they "learn in quietness" (*hesuchia,* 1 Timothy 2:9-11). Paul's idea of appropriate attire for Christian women consisted of "good deeds." Twice he mentions the importance of "propriety," which translates a word that had a technical meaning in the philosophy of Aristotle. Propriety (*sophrosyne*) was the middle road between two extremes. For example, between cowardice and foolhardiness there is the virtue of courage. Paul wanted the women to live well-balanced lives.

Women had greater freedom in Asia Minor than they did in other parts of the Roman world. We know that at least for a while the temple of Artemis had a high priestess presiding over it. Women also held public offices, though these may have been gratuitous posts given them in response to significant contributions made to local governments.

The quietness (not necessarily "silence") that Paul said should characterize a woman's demeanor when learning is the same quietude he hoped for all believers (see 1 Timothy 2:2). Paul wasn't saying women needed to shut up and listen, but they should adopt the posture of a student who listens carefully and yields to the authority of the teacher. The "submission" of the woman in this passage is the sort of respect any disciple would show to a leader and to the message of the gospel (the same Greek word is used in 2 Corinthians 9:13).

Now we come to what Paul did *not* want from the women: "I do not permit a woman to teach or to have authority over a man; she must be silent *[hesuchia]*" (1 Timothy 2:12). In English, this sentence is a strong statement. Did Paul mean to establish a universal rule, saying that there would *never* be a situation or a time in which a woman would lead or teach a man?

Common sense prompts us to ask, What's the problem with simply reading the plain meaning of the text? If the statement is clear, why dig for any other meaning? There are, however, at least two problems.

First, why would Paul establish a policy of exclusion in ministry within a community where there is "neither Jew nor Greek, slave nor free, male nor female, for you are all one in Christ Jesus" (Galatians 3:28)?

Second, Paul's words point to a meaning, but the meaning itself may be bigger than his words. For example, in 1 Timothy 2:15, Paul says women are "saved through childbearing." On the surface of the text we might think Paul is talking about spiritual salvation; he even uses the same Greek word, *sozo*. But the New Testament doesn't teach that men are saved by the atoning death of Christ while women are saved through childbearing! Paul's meaning is deeper than the words he uses. Our job is to get down to what he is actually communicating.

"I do not permit a woman to teach…a man" (1 Timothy 2:12). This statement is either conditioned by specific circumstances so that it applies only to Ephesus at that specific time, or it is universal and applies to all situations at all times. What factors would serve to qualify this statement? The list includes: Paul's intention, cultural background, historical circumstances, other biblical teaching, and specific uses of language or grammar.

Some people attempt to qualify Paul's statement by saying that the context of chapter 2 is a worship service and that Paul did not mean to prohibit women from teaching men in other settings. The problem with this view is that Paul does not mention worship services but in fact refers to "men everywhere" (2:8) or in every place lifting up holy hands. What Paul has to say in this letter about church leadership and other issues demonstrates that his definition of church was not a Sunday worship service but the everyday life of believers within a spiritual community.

On the other hand, if Paul's statement is not qualified, then there is never a time or place when women should teach men, including Bible schools and seminaries, books, Bible study guides, television, or radio. And what are we to make of Timothy's spiritual training, which he received from his mother and grandmother (see 2 Timothy 1:5)? Even though this view may seem extreme, there are people who hold that Paul is forbidding women to teach men in *any* context.

However, others understand that Paul's statement is qualified. For example, the early church father John Chrysostom initially took a strong stand against women teachers but realized that conflicted with Titus 2:3-4, where older women are admonished to train younger women. Therefore Chrysostom concluded that women could teach at home. When he came to Priscilla's role in Acts 18, he adjusted his view so that women could not teach men who were already godly and versed in the faith. Even conservative scholars today find biblical grounds for older women to teach younger women and children (as Paul directed Titus). They also believe in the validity of women serving in professorships and as conference and seminar speakers. Therefore, if Paul's statement is qualified, the questions are: What are the qualifying factors that limit the scope of this passage? How far is it to be limited?

The context of 1 Timothy and the wider context of the city of Ephesus might lead us to conclude that the passage in chapter 2 is qualified by factors that were peculiar to the cult of Artemis during Paul's lifetime. I offer this as a tentative hypothesis—it is one way of reading the historical background of 1 Timothy. Paul was dealing with a local situation that had to do with deeply entrenched customs and practices. Introducing Christianity into this pagan culture required Christian women to become grounded in the faith and not perpetuate the practices of their upbringing. This doesn't mean we can't find a broader application for all believers, both male and female. What it means is that Paul's specific concern had to do with myths and fables that exerted a strong influence in the culture that threatened the faith of the Christians in Ephesus.

We must move on. Paul told Timothy he did not permit a woman to teach or to "have authority over a man" (1 Timothy 2:12). Paul used a rare Greek word to make his point. As a rule, when Paul spoke of authority (his, God's, an apostle's), he used the word *exousia* (see, for instance, 2 Corinthians 10:8). But in this verse, Paul chose the Greek word *authenteo,* which does not appear anywhere else in the New Testament and was used infrequently in Greek literature. Therefore we must ask why Paul used this particular word. (Is it possible that a woman could exercise *exousia* over a man without exercising *authenteo?* After all, it is *authenteo* Paul prohibits, not *exousia.*)

The precise meaning of *authenteo* has been the center of much scrutiny. First, it is a rare word with a previously uncertain origin. It is quite possible that there is no way to translate into English all of what Paul meant to communicate by using this word. Second, the most important passage in Scripture relating to the involvement of women in ministry may hinge on the meaning of this rare word.

When we check a lexicon or a Bible dictionary of Greek words, we see that the definition given for *authenteo* is derived from Christian sources, dating back to the church fathers of the second or third century. The common definition is "usurp authority" or "exercise authority," but that definition came one hundred or two hundred years after Paul wrote this letter to Timothy.

Further insight into the meaning of this word has been gained through the use of the Thesaurus Linguae Graecae (TLG), a resource assembled by scholars at the University of California at Irvine. The TLG is the compilation in digital form of all existing Greek writings. This enables scholars to study the use of the word *authenteo* in nonbiblical Greek works. L. Edward Wilshire used the TLG to research roughly 314 references to *authenteo* in Greek literature, plus additional instances of its use in papyri and other literary works. He concluded that nonbiblical usage of this word at the time of Timothy conveyed the idea of murder or suicide. Wilshire's use of the TLG provided new understanding of the word's usage during the time we are studying. Earlier research had concluded that the idea of murder was *not* integral to the basic meaning of *authenteo*. The TLG proves otherwise.

The word *authenteo* was first used centuries prior to the New Testament by the greatest of all tragedy writers, Aeschylus, in connection with a sacrifice offered to none other than the goddess Artemis. In the play *Agamemnon,* the leading female character vengefully murders her husband for sacrificing their daughter to Artemis. Aeschylus may have coined the word *authenteo* to convey the unambiguous meaning "to murder with a vengeance." After Aeschylus, *authenteo* referred either to "murder" or "to die by one's own hand." In the third century A.D., Clement of Alexandria used *authenteo* in three places to mean "murderer." However, the period of time in which the meaning of *authenteo* becomes confusing for us is exactly when Paul used it.

There is a passage in the Apocrypha that makes use of *authenteo*. The Wisdom of Solomon addresses Israel's sins against God, sins that included "their works of sorcery and unholy rites, their merciless slaughter of children, and their sacrificial feasting on human flesh and blood. These initiates from the midst of a heathen cult, these parents who murder helpless lives, thou didst will to destroy by the hands of our fathers" (Wisdom 12:4-6, RSV).

The phrase "murder helpless lives" translates *authenteo* and appears in the context of "a heathen cult." This use of *authenteo* parallels the way it was used in Greek tragedies, where it appears ten times written by three different authors, and in each case it refers to the murder of an immediate family member. Could Paul have had this use of the word in mind, and if so, why?

According to ancient sources, there was a ritual practiced in the cult of Artemis in which a man was symbolically (not literally) murdered by having blood drawn from his throat. Was Paul prohibiting Christian women in Ephesus from participating in a ritual murder in the temple of Artemis? For this suggestion to be plausible we would have to know that such a ritual was so deeply ingrained in the Ephesian culture that it would be difficult even for Christians to abandon it.

There are many problems with this idea, however. What Christian community would have to be told to desist a practice of ritual murder? Also, it would hardly be necessary for Paul to tell Timothy that he disallowed such cultic activities, because Timothy would already know they were excluded. After the brouhaha recorded in Acts 19, everyone in Ephesus would be aware of Paul's attitude toward Artemis and her cult.

Is it possible that there was another practice related to the cult of Artemis that was not so violent that went by the name of *authenteo*? Perhaps Paul was mocking a cultural practice familiar to the Ephesians in much the same way that he ribbed the Cretans: "Even one of their own prophets has said, 'Cretans are always liars, evil brutes, lazy gluttons' " (Titus 1:12). We don't yet have enough evidence to answer for certain.

However, there must be some reason why Paul used this particular word. It is very likely that he had a precise meaning in mind.

The concern women had regarding childbirth, which Paul addressed in 1 Timothy 2:15, definitely had ties to the role of Artemis in providing protection for mothers while giving birth. Paul seems to be offering reassurance to the Christian women of Ephesus that when it comes time to deliver their children, God will protect them, provided they remain securely in His will. They didn't have to pay homage to Artemis to be "saved through childbearing."

The cult of Artemis remained a potent force in Ephesus for several more centuries after Christianity arrived there. In fact, it was Christianity's greatest rival. Some scholars, such as British archaeologist William Ramsay, see a direct link between the cult of Artemis and the veneration of Mary. Oddly enough, it was the Ecumenical Council of Ephesus (A.D. 431-433)—a council convened to address the Nestorian controversy regarding the nature of Jesus—that Mary was declared to be *theotokos,* "God-bearer" or "mother of God." We may also note the current Roman Catholic practice in many countries of parading adorned statues of Mary through city streets in veneration of the Virgin.

Paul illustrated (or supported, perhaps) his teaching regarding the role of women with a reference to the Old Testament, "For Adam was formed first, then Eve. And Adam was not the one deceived; it was the woman who was deceived and became a sinner" (1 Timothy 2:13-14). There are two critical points here: Adam came "first in time," and Eve was deceived whereas Adam was not.

In stressing that Adam was created first, is Paul suggesting that men have priority over women or that they are superior to them? Some people think Paul is defining an order and hierarchy that is inherent in the creation of humans. But there is nothing in the Genesis story that says Adam was first in importance. In fact, a careful study of the order of creation in Genesis 1 would suggest that being created last is the higher honor. Adam was simply around before Eve was created. But that contradicted an ancient tradition of the Anatolian Mother Goddess, Artemis Ephesia, (and other ancient myths from Canaan and Babylon that were familiar to most Jews). In those cults, the goddess existed prior to any males and gave birth to the first male. This Eastern myth would reappear in the Gnostic heresy that was to plague the church later on and was already developing at the time Paul wrote to Timothy.

When Paul said, "Adam was not the one deceived; it was the woman who was deceived," did he mean to imply that all women are by nature ill-suited for serving roles in teaching and leadership? Is Paul saying that, as a general rule, women are more susceptible to deception and Eve is evidence of a universal feminine proclivity? Some people draw this unlikely conclusion and argue that is why women should not teach men.

However, the logic of that position is undermined by three factors: First, there are several scriptural examples of men being more foolish or susceptible to deception than women, and a few cases of women having better spiritual perception than men (Deborah and Barak, Judges 4:4-9; Manoah and his wife, Judges 13:22-23; Nabal and Abigail, 1 Samuel 25:3). In fact, in the book of Proverbs, wisdom is personified as a woman (see Proverbs 8). Second, it is contrary to our own experience that in every case men are less susceptible to deception. Most every heresy known to the church has a man's name attached to it. Third, based on the view that women are more susceptible to deception, they certainly shouldn't be allowed to teach other women or children. That would be tantamount to the vulnerable leading the vulnerable.

So why did Paul point out that Eve, rather than Adam, was deceived? First, Paul did not say that women are prone to spiritual deception. Neither was he appealing to a divine ordering (or hierarchy) of the sexes. The fact that Eve was meant to be a "help" suitable for Adam certainly does not assign her a lesser importance. In many Old Testament references, the same Hebrew word *(ayzer)* is used of God in relationship to His people, "We wait in hope for the LORD; he is our help *[ayzer]* and our shield" (Psalm 33:20).

Paul made reference to Adam and Eve simply because they were the first man and woman. The biblical history of Adam and Eve contradicted the tradition of the Anatolian Artemis of Ephesus.[5] To generalize Paul's statement to all women in all times does a disservice to the historical context in which Timothy lived and carried out his ministry.

Given the historical background of 1 Timothy, including the influence of the cult of Artemis, we could possibly interpret 1 Timothy 2:8-15 in the following way: Paul's teaching ministry destabilized the devotion to Artemis in Ephesus, thus threatening the livelihood of those whose businesses were derived from the pagan temple. Paul's intent in 1 Timothy was to undermine the myths that supported the economic, political, and religious beliefs held by the Ephesians. In taking a swipe at the "old wives' tales" and specific rituals related to Artemis, Paul sought to emphasize what until then had been a marginalized Christian worldview. At the same time, he was redefining "reality" (or spirituality) for the Ephesians; he was rewriting their history by acquainting them with the historical teaching of Genesis. He was also steering women away from a practice relating to the Artemis cult that was deeply ingrained in their local culture.

CONCLUSION

Where are we to land as we view Paul's teaching in its historical, religious, and cultural context? Can we safely conclude that the teaching is limited to the challenges of living faithfully as a Christian amid the rank paganism of this Artemis-worshiping culture? Here is my personal interpretation:

- The rituals and practices of the Artemis cult were so ingrained in the culture of Ephesus that Christians there needed strong teaching to open their eyes to the pagan meaning of these common practices. Young women were so accustomed to presenting themselves in the Artemisium before getting married or delivering a child—as their mothers and grandmothers had—that they didn't think twice about the implications of those acts. These pagan rituals posed a real threat to the faith of the Ephesian believers. Christian women in the region had to be warned away from those things.

• Paul's instructions to Timothy regarding the role of women not teaching or *authentein* men have a specific and local reference to ancient Ephesus and were never meant to be a general prohibition against women in leadership and teaching roles. Because of the influence of Artemis worship, Paul found it necessary to provide detailed teaching to correct the specific challenges faced by Christians in that city.

The previous points reflect my personal belief, and I'd like to be able to tell you that these interpretations are unassailable. But I don't have enough information to confidently assert that this is the truest and best interpretation. However, there is more than enough historical data to seriously question the hyperliteral interpretations of 1 Timothy 2. We need to be cautious about using this passage to legislate contemporary church practice, especially the practice of exclusion, until we have enough evidence to draw a more reliable conclusion.

As you research the historical background of certain passages, new vistas of understanding and insight will open up. The context lying behind a passage is a crucial piece in solving the puzzle of its meaning. At the very least, we may learn how to become more patient, compassionate, and mature as we wait for the light of historical research to shine ever more brightly on the biblical text.

CHAPTER 8

RESIDENT ALIENS

Paying Attention to
Cultural Realities

Ask me something specific about President Eisenhower's or President Kennedy's administrations and you'll get nothing more than a blank stare. But ask me about Saturday-morning cartoons in the sixties and there won't be many questions I can't answer. When you think about all the current-event articles I had to clip out of the newspaper and bring to school, it's sad that not one of them had the slightest effect on my education. Even sadder is the fact that I can remember the name of Tom Terrific's cartoon "wonder dog" featured on *Captain Kangaroo.*[1]

A few years ago a Los Angeles television station began to rebroadcast the old Dick Tracy cartoons. I was amused to find that the stories and animation entertained my children just as they had me years earlier. However, within a few weeks, *Dick Tracy* was yanked off the air in response to the outcry of ethnic groups. It seems that certain characters in the cartoons were portrayed as racial stereotypes.

I had watched *Dick Tracy* religiously all those years ago, and it never occurred to me that the program promoted an imperialistic model of Western culture. That may sound like an attempt at sarcasm, but I'm completely serious. In the last two decades of the twentieth century, many scholars have opened our eyes to the essential bias of Western civilization in its literature, art, and popular culture.

For many years, the United States and Western Europe perceived themselves at the center of world civilization and human progress—every other nation represented the "uncivilized other." If Europeans and North Americans assumed that theirs were the most advanced cultures, then their art and science had universal application as the spearhead of progress for *all* humanity. Thus local art forms and the customs of "less-developed" nations were pushed to the margins.

THE BIG IDEA:

Literature can be used like a magnifying glass to scrutinize the ways a dominant culture suppresses, oppresses, and exploits other cultures. When we read biblical texts, this perspective can help us discern the tension between the culture of the world and God's people, how the world pressures believers to conform, and how believers resist that pressure.

In Western literature, are non-Europeans described in the complexity, beauty, and wisdom of their own art and culture, or are they depicted according to Western caricatures? Are there universal ideals or unvarying principles that enable us to determine that the literature of one culture is superior to the literature of another? These are samples of the questions that arise when we recognize the influence of cultural realities—the ways one culture is represented by the media, literature, and art of another culture. Ethnic groups and subcultures sometimes suffer from prejudice, oppression, exploitation, and ridicule. A foreign culture is rarely judged by its own standards. Thus social and political problems are perpetuated in print, entertainment, and other cultural expressions.

THE VIEW FROM THE MARGINS

These questions reflect real concerns among scholars who analyze the dominance of Western nations in the literary world. (This concern extends as well into the fields of philosophy, science, and mass media.) Some of these researchers have written from the margins of Western culture, being themselves immigrants to Western society. Their views and theories regarding literature are referred to as *postcolonial*.

For a long period of history, European empires—primarily England, Spain, France, and Holland—exercised direct political control over other, less-developed countries ("less developed" mostly in terms of the natural sciences and technology). The nature of these colonial relationships was such that the governing nation typically accrued economic or military benefits at the expense of the colonized nation. The ruling nation considered its own citizens and society to be more "advanced" than the colonized culture. An inherent racism also was characteristic of the colonial enterprise, so that in many instances, even those native to a culture attributed greater prestige to the culture and language of the colonizing nation.

Postcolonialism marks the decline of European rule and the effort of many nations in Africa, Asia, and the Caribbean to rediscover their earlier cultures, evaluate their political options, and form new national identities. Postcolonial literary theory, therefore, demonstrates two concerns. The first is to find a method of interpretation that identifies how one culture is dominated and marginalized in the written works of another culture. The second is to identify the unique contributions that have been made by cultures outside of Western civilization. These contributions would include Native American, African American, and Latino works of literature and art that have been produced in the United States.

IS POSTCOLONIALISM BIBLICAL?

It's easy to think of postcolonialism as a concept that is useful only in academic circles. However, while the concept and terminology may be of recent origin, the concerns about colonialism are actually central to the Scriptures. Israel became a nation when its people were still enslaved by Egypt. Hundreds of years later, they became colonial exiles in Babylon and Persia. After the collapse of Israel's monarchy, foreigners were colonized in the northern tribes of Israel. And skipping forward to the New Testament, Jews were living under the political domination of Rome at the time of Jesus. This explains why the basic tenets of postcolonial interpretation apply to large portions of the Bible. The same principles also apply to the lives of Christians, since our calling is to be *in* the world but not *of* it. We must resist being colonized by the world's value system.

The fact that for most of its history Israel was not a significant world power means that the people of Israel were subject to political and cultural domination. This is one reason why the worship of other gods was such a threat. The common belief during the Old Testament period was that if one army prevailed over another, it could well be that the victor's gods were more powerful (see 2 Chronicles 28:23). Israel's experience with colonialism was a spiritual battle against forces that either seduced or coerced the Israelites into the worship of other gods.

Paying attention to cultural realities can help us identify the ways Israel was exploited by other nations. In addition, paying attention to cultural realities can give us a greater appreciation for the craft of the biblical writers. Texts that may confuse a reader who is an English speaker yield a wealth of spiritual insight when read according to their own rules and conventions. There are aspects of Hebrew literature and New Testament writings that are beautiful and creative when read in their cultural context.

YES, THERE ARE LIABILITIES

In the academic world, postcolonialism is decidedly political. Our suspicions are justified when the Bible is used to support political ideologies. But that doesn't mean this method can't also be used as a valid tool for understanding Scripture. To the degree that postcolonialism gives us a greater awareness of the way powerful regimes exploit less-developed nations, it's a useful tool. For example, postcolonial theory when applied to the Bible may enlighten us to some of the problems we face living in a consumer culture.

The imperatives of the Bible have to do with social, relational, moral, and spiritual action. I don't believe the Bible should be used to support political ideologies, either to the right or the left. There are people all along the political spectrum, from neo-Marxists to the Ku Klux Klan, who want to claim biblical backing for their philosophies. But the study of cultural realities in Scripture cannot in good conscience be used to help build a political platform.

There is also the danger of romanticizing other cultures so that they seem to hold the keys to happiness. The romantic image of the "noble savage," the enlightened mystic, the gentle native living a harmonious existence with nature and God (or gods) are all prettified pictures that mask harsher realities. Maybe the West should not insist on leading the East, but the East is just as ill-prepared to lead the West.

A useful application of the tools of postcolonial interpretation is to apply it wherever the specific issue of oppression, racism, exclusion, exile, or international conflict occurs. Any biblical book written during or after Israel's exile in Babylon and Persia would provide fertile ground for studying the cultural realities related to those texts (Ezra, Ezekiel, Daniel, Nehemiah, and others). There are also contexts in the New Testament in which Hebrew and Hellenic cultures collide in ways that lend themselves to cultural investigation. This method of interpretation is perfectly suited to those biblical texts.

WHERE TO FIND THE CULTURAL REALITIES

Here are a number of questions that will help us search for the cultural realities that lie behind the text of Scripture.

Who has the power? How does the text reinforce the authority and prejudice of the identifiable power structure? How does the text destabilize or subvert the power structure? How are people outside the power structure marked as being "different"?

Which group is dominant? Is there one certain race, culture, or class that dominates another? If so, who would be defined as the outsider or foreigner? How is racial identity threatened or protected? How are the nondominant people controlled, marginalized, or excluded from power? Are they in any way stereotyped by the dominant culture?

Which group is subordinated? As we study Scripture, we are specifically concerned with the way that Jews and Christians are marginalized by a dominant power. But we must also accept the fact that sometimes Israel and the church need to be confronted regarding their treatment of the stranger or the less-fortunate person (see James 2:1-9). How are the people of God challenged to view their own culture or behavior as being oppressive?

What are the pertinent themes? Look for themes such as "homeland," "scattered people," and "exile," and analyze the role of these themes in advancing the story's plot. Are there instances of a nondominant people surrendering to their oppressors? Are there instances of resistance to the dominant political or religious system, such as the Hebrew midwives' disobedience to Pharaoh's command in Exodus 1?

Who are the exiles? In certain texts we will look for such things as what it means to be a Hebrew in Egypt, a Jew in Babylon, or a Christian in Rome.

CASE STUDY: DANIEL IN EXILE

The issues of exile and foreign cultures appear in the first few verses of the book of Daniel. It's also interesting to note that in the original language, only half the book is written in Hebrew. The other half is written in Aramaic, the dominant language in the Gentile world during the time of the Babylonian and Persian Empires.

The book of Daniel is as much Babylonian as it is Hebrew—it is set in Babylon, not Judah; it records episodes from the lives of Babylonian and Persian kings, not Israel's kings; and it reveals the future of the Gentile kingdoms, not the nation of Israel. If language and culture are the visible expressions of a community, then the book of Daniel reveals a people with an identity crisis. What language are they to speak and whose story will they tell?

Daniel's story is remarkable because, on the one hand, he cooperated with the empire, submitted to its laws, and worked on behalf of a pagan king. On the other hand, he and his friends refused to be assimilated into the imperial culture. They did not "defile" themselves by bowing down to pagan images or by ceasing their prayers and devotion to Yahweh. Their story demonstrates how it is possible to remain faithful to God while living under the jurisdiction of a pagan, foreign culture.

> In the third year of the reign of Jehoiakim king of Judah, Nebuchadnezzar king of Babylon came to Jerusalem and besieged it. And the Lord delivered Jehoiakim king of Judah into his hand, along with some of the articles from the temple of God. These he carried off to the temple of his god in Babylon and put in the treasure house of his god. (Daniel 1:1-2)

Babylon did not defeat Jerusalem, but "the Lord delivered" Jerusalem and its king into the hand of Nebuchadnezzar. Now Israel would have to "serve foreigners in a land not [their] own" (Jeremiah 5:19). This was a fate the people of Judah could not escape or resist, because God had already determined it. The atmosphere of the first chapter is characterized by inevitability, as Israel is forced to accept the conditions of a new life.

What were those conditions? One is the possibility of what theologian

Walter Brueggemann called "success through conformity."[2] That is to say, if Daniel and his friends agreed to submit to the Babylonian system, they could count on a comfortable and well-rewarded life. The complication is that conforming to Babylonian culture meant compromising their own culture. Living as a faithful Jew in Babylon meant walking a high wire where one had to be perfectly balanced or fall from favor, either in the eyes of the king of Babylon or with the God of Abraham, Isaac, and Jacob.

> Then the king ordered Ashpenaz, chief of his court officials, to bring in some of the Israelites from the royal family and the nobility—young men without any physical defect, handsome, showing aptitude for every kind of learning, well informed, quick to understand, and qualified to serve in the king's palace. He was to teach them the language and literature of the Babylonians. The king assigned them a daily amount of food and wine from the king's table. They were to be trained for three years, and after that they were to enter the king's service. (Daniel 1:3-5)

In exercising his sovereignty over the Jews, Nebuchadnezzar requisitioned into his service the best and the brightest of their youth. The most talented and promising young men of Judah would be groomed to serve Babylon. But to do this, they would have to be indoctrinated into Babylonian culture and literature. While receiving a world-class education, these young men would feel not only the pressure of the king's power to conform but also the seductions of royal cuisine and luxuries. And if there was no more temple, no more Jerusalem, no more monarchy of Israel or Judah, what was left to defend and uphold? They were in the right place for rationalizing moral and spiritual defection from Israel's religion if they chose to accommodate themselves to the Babylonian worldview and lifestyle.

> Among these were some from Judah: Daniel, Hananiah, Mishael
> and Azariah. The chief official gave them new names: to Daniel,
> the name Belteshazzar; to Hananiah, Shadrach; to Mishael,
> Meshach; and to Azariah, Abednego. (Daniel 1:6-7)

To appreciate the magnitude of coercion implied here, we have to understand the significance of a person's name in Old Testament times. Parents gave much thought to their children's names, which was considered to be nearly synonymous with their identity and destiny. In some cases, God intervened and gave names to people, because whoever named a person *defined* that person.

When the chief official gave new names to Daniel and his friends, he acted as representative of the empire. The former Hebrew names Daniel, Hananiah, Mishael, and Azariah connected them to the nation and God of Israel. So Babylon, the colonial power, sought to redefine them, change their identities, and erase their past loyalties. Daniel's Hebrew name meant "God is judge." His identity, therefore, was bound up in his relationship and service to God. The chief officer, however, named him after one of Babylon's gods, "Bel" (or "Lord"). Daniel's new name was intended to tear his destiny away from Israel and attach it to Babylon.

The tension between culture and God is an issue that believers have found relevant in every age. In fact, perhaps the only time in history when there was little or no tension between culture and God was when Israel sojourned in the wilderness under the administration of Moses. Otherwise, the instructions of Paul have always been applicable to believers, "Do not conform any longer to the pattern of this world" (Romans 12:2).

Daniel resisted—both passively and actively—the pressure to accept a pagan identity. The passive resistance is reflected in his memoirs, where he constantly refers to himself in the third person but never once uses his Babylonian name. Daniel was so effective in retaining his original identity and therefore his loyalty to God that by the time the Persians defeated the

Babylonians and subsumed Daniel under their administration, he was referred to only as Daniel.

His resistance was also active (or activist):

> But Daniel resolved not to defile himself with the royal food and wine, and he asked the chief official for permission not to defile himself this way. Now God had caused the official to show favor and sympathy to Daniel. (Daniel 1:8-9)

We need to remember that Daniel belonged to a defeated people who lived on the margins of society. Although he was privileged to live and work among the king's viziers, he was still a foreigner—not to mention that he was on probation. He could be sent back to the margins of society for any little misstep. Daniel was a foreigner being pressured to adopt the pagan empire as his own, yet he dared to stand apart and fought to preserve his religious and cultural identity.

RESISTING THE PRESSURE TO CONFORM

What was the problem with the royal provisions? Nothing, as far as any level-headed Babylonian was concerned. But the problem for a Hebrew youth derived from the law of God regarding clean and unclean foods. If Daniel were to eat the king's cuisine, no matter how nutritious and pleasurable to consume, he would have been "defiled" according to the regulations of the Mosaic Law.

Daniel believed that the royal food and wine posed a threat to his integrity, that it would constitute an unacceptable compromise. He did not have two identities—one Babylonian and the other Hebrew. If he were to allow himself to be dichotomized, then he would be neither Jewish nor Babylonian. In the words of James, leader of the Jerusalem church, he would be a "double-minded man" who is "unstable in all he does" (James 1:8).

The solution to dichotomy is integrity, a word that finds its root in *integer,* a whole number, "anything complete in itself." Perhaps this is what the poet meant when he prayed, "Give me an undivided heart, that I may fear your name" (Psalm 86:11). If Daniel allowed himself to be "defiled," redefined, or named by Babylon, then he would compromise his integrity, lose his identity, and fail to realize his destiny.

Walter Brueggemann points out that the word *defile* "contains a first hint of a pejorative comment against the empire. Daniel reckons that the imperial diet will make him unacceptable and distort his person."[3] Until the moment that this word occurs—and Daniel's resolve not to eat the king's food—there is no apparent tension in the text regarding a Jew serving in Nebuchadnezzar's palace. These were simply the circumstances that had fallen to Israel. But in verse 8, an underlying conflict emerges, and Daniel must be resolute. (We might also notice that suspense is introduced into the narrative when Daniel suggests a contest between the "young men" who ate the royal food and himself and his companions.)

Further study in Daniel will demonstrate that the tension between the Jewish characters and the reigning empire surfaces and subsides in various episodes. The arrogant Nebuchadnezzar had to learn that "the Most High is sovereign over the kingdoms of men" (4:17); Belshazzar, Nebuchadnezzar's son, had to learn that the God he had blasphemed held the king's life in His hand (see 5:23); and the Persian king, Darius, had to discover a law higher than decrees put in writing so that they cannot be broken—"in accordance with the laws of the Medes and Persians" (6:8).

We might ask how a young man such as Daniel found it possible to live in a pagan culture such as Babylon without compromising his faith. The answer appears in chapter 6, after King Darius was talked into issuing a decree that prohibited anyone from praying to any god or man other than the king. How did Daniel respond to this new law?

Now when Daniel learned that the decree had been published, he went home to his upstairs room where the windows opened toward Jerusalem. Three times a day he got down on his knees and prayed, giving thanks to his God, just as he had done before. (Daniel 6:10)

Daniel lived in Babylon, but not as a Babylonian. How did he resist the pressure to conform? He opened his windows toward Jerusalem. In other words, he lived in Babylon but with an orientation toward Jerusalem. In fact, he was careful to reorient himself to the holy city three times a day. No doubt beginning his day, ending his day, and bisecting his day with prayer toward Jerusalem helped him to remember who he was and whom he served. His identity was secure because he grounded it in a reality other than Babylon.

The book of Daniel, when viewed from the perspective of its cultural realities, reveals how believers are pushed and pulled when they are minority members of a pagan society. Daniel also provides an excellent example of resistance to those cultural forces that pressure believers to conform (although Daniel was never a political activist). How do people in parallel situations maintain a steady focus on their true identity and find the power to resist? By constantly orienting themselves to God who stands outside the dominant culture, who is more powerful than the imperial decree, and who calls His people to be "willing to give up their lives rather than serve or worship any god except their own God" (Daniel 3:28).

I have no doubt that Christians can benefit greatly from using the tools of postcolonial theory as they read the prophetic book of Daniel. We, too, feel the pressure to conform to our world, which will redefine who we are if we don't anchor our identity in something (or Someone) outside our culture. If we can discipline ourselves to constantly reorient our hearts toward Jesus, then we will receive the strength to fulfill His prayer that we would be in the world but not of it (see John 17:15-16).

A number of other portions of Scripture, including many in the New Testament, yield rich insights when you pay attention to the cultural realities that are revealed in the text. Turning to the book of Acts, we find the interesting and complicated relationship of Gentile and "open" Jewish Christians to the strict, "closed" Jewish Christians who believed that a person could not be saved unless he was first "circumcised, according to the custom taught by Moses" (Acts 15:1). The dominant religious system, which strictly held to the laws of Judaism, exerted enough power that even some Christians collapsed under the pressure to conform.

How can we identify similar pressures today, and where will we find the power and motivation not to compromise our faith? Those are the questions we must answer as we use the tool of postcolonial theory to uncover deeper truths about living faithfully in a foreign, sometimes hostile, culture.

LECTIO DIVINA

Paying Attention to the Inner Voice

When I was hard at work one day, thinking on the spiritual work needful for God's servants, four such spiritual works came to my mind, these being: reading; meditation; prayer; contemplation. This is the ladder for those in cloisters, and for others in the world who are God's Lovers, by means of which they can climb from earth to heaven. It is a marvelously tall ladder, but with just four rungs, the one end standing on the ground, the other thrilling into the clouds and showing the climber heavenly secrets.

GUIGO II, SCALA PARADISO

The mystic I just quoted, Guigo II, was a twelfth-century Carthusian monk—that is, he belonged to a strict religious order in Chartreuse, France. Basing his theme on the ladder in Jacob's dream, Guigo wanted to provide spiritual pilgrims—"God's lovers"—as well as monks and nuns a guide for receiving divine insights. His work is also known as *Scala Claustralium (A Ladder of Monastics)* and by its English title, *A Ladder of Four Rungs.*[1]

Guigo's short work presents a prayerful way to listen to God through the Scriptures. He weaves together a spiritual exercise of four braids consisting of *lectio* (reading), *meditatio* (meditation), *oratio* (prayer), and *contemplatio* (contemplation). Although some think of these four activities as steps or stages, they are more like alternating means of opening one's heart to communion with God. Together they form the basis of the *lectio divina*, or sacred reading of Scripture.

Unlike the subjects covered in the earlier chapters of this book, *lectio* is not a method of biblical interpretation but rather a way of putting our ear close to the Bible to hear God's voice speak directly to us. This is a spiritual experience, a means of encountering God, rather than a formal study. *Lectio* helps us attune our hearts to God's voice, and Scripture becomes the instrument by which He speaks. We are listening for God's voice with our spirits rather than straining to understand the Bible with our minds.

Lectio divina does not involve the close, careful reading of the text that is required for interpretive methods. The word *lectio* means reading, but this spiritual discipline is really more about listening. Our concern here is not with the way words are put together to produce meaning, but with the words themselves and how God might use them to awaken something within us. *Lectio* is a means of opening our hearts to receive God's grace.

Lectio approaches the Bible as you would a love letter. Love letters are not written to be critically analyzed, but so the reader can hear the voice and heart of the lover. That is the purpose of this spiritual discipline, to hear the voice and heart of God. When we engage in *lectio,* we believe God is immediately accessible to our hearts, minds, and spirits.

Reading seeks, meditation finds, prayer asks, contemplation feels.[2]

To practice the four activities of sacred reading requires that we learn to listen to God through Scripture and through our heart as it responds to the words of the Bible. The Spirit of God speaks to us both through the Bible and through an inner voice. Something in the text will strike a chord within us, and we must be able to recognize the moment that it happens.

No part of the process is forced. Instead, our reading, meditation, prayer, and contemplation are passive exercises in which we rest in God's goodness and grace and *allow* Him to speak. We will seek to relax into the Bible, waiting for God to speak and responding to the gentle impulses of His Spirit.

THE BIG IDEA:

Lectio divina is a spiritual exercise that consists of prayerfully holding a word, phrase, or verse of Scripture in our hearts until God speaks to us through it. The movement of *lectio* is from Word to mind, from mind to heart, from heart to spirit.

The optimal way to approach *lectio* is with a warm and deep affection for Scripture. We need to be able to say with Jeremiah, "When your words came, I ate them; they were my joy and my heart's delight, for I bear your name, O LORD God Almighty" (Jeremiah 15:16). If we feel a desperate hunger to feed on God's Word, if we hang on the "gracious words" that fall from Jesus' lips (see Luke 4:22), then we have the proper frame of mind to hear the voice of our Beloved speak to us.

While it is referred to by its Latin title, *lectio divina* is not a Catholic practice that Protestants should be wary of. The sacred reading of Scripture dates back at least to the third century and has been advocated by such Protestant luminaries as Martin Luther and John Wesley. We all can cultivate the quietness and concentration required for this type of listening.

READING WITH THE HEART

There are at least two ways to read the Bible: We can read with our minds or with our hearts. To read with the mind is to "diligently study the Scriptures" (John 5:39) by searching, examining, analyzing, and drawing conclusions. Reading with the heart is a way of allowing Scripture to enter us, opening windows so that God's words can unfold in our hearts, giving light and "understanding to the simple" (Psalm 119:130). The first approach is cognitive, the second is affective or contemplative.

Proverbs 3:5 draws a contrast between trusting God with our *hearts* and leaning on our own understanding. Generally, our intellect serves us well in the study of Scripture, but there are times when it can get in the way of our trust. We can know the meaning of a passage but still doubt. We can believe the truth of a verse, but while putting it into practice we still fail to trust God. *Lectio* requires a whole-hearted trust in the Lord.

What prevents us from hearing God's voice every time we read the Bible? Often, it's our tendency to either theologize or sermonize as we read. I've known Christians who study the Bible for the express purpose of improving their arguments when debating other people. When we read the Bible with this sort of cerebral intent, it is not surprising that we miss whatever *personal* message God may want to deliver.

We sermonize our Bible reading whenever we read a passage and then "preach" at ourselves. We read Scripture as if every verse were an exhortation meant to produce conviction. We are so used to reading the Bible this way that when we come to the place where Jesus called Levi to follow Him, and we read that "Levi got up, left everything and followed him" (Luke 5:28), we hear a nagging voice asking us, "Are *you* willing to leave everything to follow Jesus?" This tendency often perverts the intent of Scripture. Perhaps it goes back to the way guilt was used to manipulate us as children in Sunday school, but many of us are much too eager to embrace condemnation and a list of "I should" and "I ought."

To sermonize our Bible reading is basically a self-centered act, as if every verse in the Bible were about *me*. When the gospel writers tell the story of Levi's call, they do not add this exhortation: "Are *you* willing to leave everything?" Rather, they are telling us something about Jesus. They are telling us He is a person who draws other people to Himself, and His appeal is so great that people are willing to leave everything to go with Him. We need to read the text with the intent of seeing what it has to say about Jesus. *Lectio divina* is a remedy for the kind of reading that condemns but never consoles, that wounds and never heals, that informs but never transforms.

To read with the heart is to suspend critical thinking and let the words flow into our souls. If we ask Jesus to speak to us, then read the words of Scripture as if they were His voice, there will be words that touch us with a special urgency. Intellectually, we may reason our way around what our hearts hear, but if we stay with it, eventually our minds will catch up and support the thoughts that Jesus gives us.

A Necessary Caveat

Seeing that we have come across so many Latin words in this chapter, I thought a caveat would be appropriate. Suppose you are engaged in *lectio* and suddenly you are overwhelmed with a flood of emotions. A long-ago pain is remembered, and you instantly see the negative influence it has had in your life. At the same time, you realize you have been set free from its power and control. And all of this followed your meditation on a single word of Scripture. What is so wrong with that?

Nothing really, except the possibility that you mistake your experience for a genuine encounter with God. The way *lectio* is frequently taught today it is not only a spiritual exercise but also a therapeutic way of accessing the unconscious—a form of self-hypnosis. It is possible to produce a powerful experience—a catharsis—that is entirely explainable in psychological terms. Catharsis can occur in humans apart from any belief in or reliance on God. To have an encounter with God is far more than an emotional event.

A related concern is that the word or phrase we choose for our meditation is something that our unconscious latches on to, but is not the message God intended for us. A word in the text may impress us, not because God wants to speak to us through that word, but because there is something in our own history that associates itself with it. The danger is that we'll assume God is directing us because of the psychological force of a word, when, in reality, our own hidden thoughts are leading the exercise. *Lectio* is about listening to God and not merely the contents of our unconscious mind.

How then should we proceed? First, we need to acknowledge the connection between our mind and spirit. There isn't a brain surgeon or scanning device in the world that can detect where the mind leaves off and the spirit begins. God can minister to us through unconscious thoughts that rise in response to the Scripture as well as He can through the thoughts He plants in our minds. While an authentic spiritual experience is more than a therapeutic event, a psychological breakthrough can nevertheless be part of our spiritual experience. The crucial factor is that whatever our experience, we seek above all else to approach God and surrender ourselves to Him and His will. God's work in our spirit will not bypass our mind or leave it unchanged.

Second, in *lectio* one of the first things we do is ask the Holy Spirit to guide our exercise. Think about Jesus' promise in Luke 11:

> Which of you fathers, if your son asks for a fish, will give him a snake instead? Or if he asks for an egg, will give him a scorpion? If you then, though you are evil, know how to give good gifts to your children, how much more will your Father in heaven give the Holy Spirit to those who ask him! (Luke 11:11-13)

We need to engage in sacred reading with a confidence that God's Spirit will speak to us and lead us in the direction that pleases Him most.

Third, *lectio divina* requires us to pass the insights and intuitions that come to us through several tests. Because we are prone to project our deep desires into the text, we have to constantly guard our sacred reading. To that end, we learn to apply the test of Scripture interpreted according to the historical-grammatical method as honestly and accurately as possible. Then there is the test of spiritual discernment. There are also the tests of common sense, of what is good or beneficial, and the test of godly men and women whose counsel we trust.

If you think that God has spoken to you, but the message seems a little strange, talk it over with your pastor, priest, or other leader in your church. *Lectio* is not meant to reveal hidden or secret meanings of the Bible, but to allow God to speak to you in a personal way. Nothing that God speaks to you during your sacred reading should be considered an inspired revelation; it has the same status as any idea or impulse that comes to you with the possibility of being sent by God. You will find that most insights that come to you in *lectio* are of a personal nature and have to do with your relationship with Jesus and others.

LECTIO DIVINA IN PRACTICE

Reading puts as it were whole food into your mouth; meditation chews it and breaks it down; prayer finds its savor; contemplation is the sweetness that so delights and strengthens.[3]

Lectio divina poses a great challenge because to be able to hear the "still, small voice" of God, we must be able to *pay attention*. With all the distractions, our short attention span, and the endless stream of sound from televisions, radios, traffic, and lawn mowers, the ability to concentrate is a skill we have to cultivate. Otherwise, any attempt to maintain the focus in reading, meditation, and prayer will be foiled. To assist our concentration, we can learn to do as David, who said, "But I have stilled and quieted my soul; like a weaned child with its mother, like a weaned child is my soul within me" (Psalm 131:2). The *lectio* begins with learning how to rest.

There are many ways to prepare your mind and body for serious concentration. From the monastic traditions, believers have adopted the "Jesus Prayer" in which a person concentrates on breathing—taking deep, slow breaths—and praying "Lord Jesus Christ, Son of God" with every inhalation and "Have mercy on me" with every exhalation. Some people simply breathe deeply and at the end of every exhalation say the name "Jesus."

The quickest and easiest way to relax the mind is to go through the *back door,* that is, your body. Our brains are in dynamic communication with the rest of the body. Mental stress causes muscle tension, and it is not unusual to develop knots in your shoulders and neck. This is one of the ways our brains prepare our bodies for action, by triggering our nervous system. But these brain and body connections work the other way as well. Our brains respond to physical sickness, injury, caffeine consumption, and medication. If we can address the stress or agitation we feel in our body, we can also calm our brains.

What follows is a standard technique for relaxation:

- Begin with prayer. Call on the name of Jesus, and as you do, imagine God shrouding you in His presence. Rest in God's presence.
- Slowly take a deep breath, knowing that the Spirit (*pneuma,* breath, wind) is like the air that is all around you and enters you as you breathe.
- Hold your breath for five seconds, and as you do, tighten your face muscles and keep them tight. Relax your face as you exhale.
- Take another deep breath and raise your shoulders, tightening the muscles in your neck and upper back. Again, hold them tight for five seconds, then relax and exhale.
- Continue doing this, working your way down the rest of your body. You might even want to say something to each muscle group like, "The peace of the Lord be with you." I know this might sound a little strange, but we hardly know how to enjoy the "peace that passes all understanding" in actual practice.
- Tilt your head from side to side, and nod it back and forth (do *not* roll your head or use your hand to make "adjustments" to your neck). Rotate your wrists and ankles. Imagine that you are working out all the stress in them.
- Inhale, exhale, and call on the Lord simply by saying the name of Jesus. If you experience the sudden intrusion of an unwanted thought, either calmly give it to God in prayer or write it down so you can deal with it later.

- Sing a worshipful song or hymn. By worshiping God in this way, you turn your attention toward Him and His awesome nature.

Eventually you will be able to relax without taking so many steps, and you'll be amazed how much clearer your thoughts are for reading and meditation. Now we are ready to begin. Breathe deep, relax, sit up straight, and pray, "Spirit of God, please lead me to what you want me to see in this text. Infiltrate my mind, open my eyes, and enlighten me through the Scripture that I read." Next, choose your reading carefully. One option is to work your way through a book of the Bible, which has the added value of always presenting your next passage for reading. The Gospels are excellent material for *lectio*. But don't attempt to read long passages. Rather, read units of thoughts—which are marked by subheadings in most versions of the Bible. You will probably read no more than ten or fifteen verses.

The purpose of your first reading is to determine the passage's overall theme or idea. Do not analyze the text, look for lessons, or read any marginal notes or cross references. Simply look at the text as if it were a painting and you wanted to enjoy its colors and textures. There is no need to wrack your brain trying to understand every verse.

Once you are fairly clear on what the text is about, read it again slowly, one word at a time. This time, look for any word, phrase, or idea (perhaps a theme that is repeated) that catches your attention. If you find something, continue reading to the end of the passage and see if that word or phrase is still with you. If it is, think about it for a moment.

This is where you will begin meditation. Repeat the word or phrase in your mind. Sometimes it will unfold like the petals of a flower, and you will begin to discover its connections to other issues in your life. Other times it will simply sit in your mind. If you think it is hiding something important from you, quietly and calmly pray for God to elaborate, to give you a better understanding of what He wants to show you.

Slowly read the passage again and see if the same word or phrase still speaks to you more than anything else in the text. If a different word or phrase makes a stronger impression, then switch to the new phrase. Otherwise, continue with the original thought. Breathe deeply, sense God's presence with you, and hold the word or phrase in your mind the way you melt hard candy in your mouth. Roll it around and let it dissolve in your thoughts.

As you concentrate on the words you have chosen (or that have chosen you), ask what kind of emotion they evoke. You are holding God's Word in your heart, and He is using it to draw to the surface issues He wants to address, problems He wants to solve, maladies He wants to heal. If your mind wanders, repeat the word or phrase a few times. Our intellect clamors so loudly most of the time that we never hear our heart. Listening "from the neck down," as one of my friends puts it, is a way of listening to God speak around our intellectual defenses.

At this point ask: What does God want me to do with this insight? What is He asking of me? There is no good reason to try to hear God speak unless we intend to obey Him. In fact, in the original languages of both the Old and New Testaments, the word *hear* is related to the word *obey.* God will speak to those who are willing to do as He says. You may have to wait for a response, but that is part of the spiritual exercise (see Psalm 27:14).

You are now ready to respond to God, to answer Him. Whatever you have thought about, discovered, or felt during your meditation now becomes the theme of your prayer. If you feel like He's calling you to make some kind of change, ask Him for His help. If it seems He wants to heal a wound, surrender to His work and tell Him you welcome His touch. If you hear Him encouraging you with His love, then allow your spirit to be lifted and built up in joy. Most of all, thank God for speaking to you, for loving you, and for showing you His infinite mercy and grace.

Breathe deeply again and rest in God's presence. There will be moments when you become so acutely aware of His presence it will seem like you can stretch out your hand and touch His face. Other times, you will sense nothing. That is normal, but rest in His presence anyway. We are like children playing in ocean waves. Sometimes the waves retreat from us so fast we can't catch them. Other times they wash over us with such force that they knock us down. Likewise, the absence and presence of God serve their own purposes in helping us grow in our relationship to Him.

Some people are opposed to writing down what they receive during their sacred reading—as if journaling were a different sort of exercise, separate from *lectio*. But it's a good idea to keep some kind of record of what God has shown you. If the lesson was important, then you don't want to forget it. You may be able to return to these thoughts at some future time and once again be inspired by them. Writing down the words you meditated on and the thoughts and feelings they evoked is another way of thinking about and working through them. At any rate, as you practice the sacred reading of Scripture, I believe you will hear God speak to you in such a significant way that you will want to capture it in writing.

I would like to end this chapter with a prayer:

Lord God, Maker of heaven and earth,
We thank You for the gift of Scripture.
You have revealed to us, not only the truth,
The way of righteousness, and the path of life,
But You have also revealed Yourself,
So that we might know You and live with You forever.
Lord, Your Word is eternal.
After heaven and earth have passed away,
After the last star has flickered out,
Your words will continue to stand;
Reliable, trustworthy, and true.
We ask You, Father,
To give us eyes to see and ears to hear
Every time we open the Bible.
Lead us to the truths You want us to learn,
The deeds You want us to perform,

The life You want us to live.
Enlighten us, encourage us, correct us, and train us
According to the Scriptures.
Keep us in Your Word, and lock Your Word in our hearts,
So that our minds are illumined by it,
Our hearts are transformed by it,
Our spirits are renewed by it,
And our behavior is shaped by it.
May the mercy of God our Father,
The truth of Jesus Christ His Son,
And the love of the Holy Spirit,
Be made real in our lives through Your eternal Word;
Both now and forever more.
Amen.

CHAPTER 10

THE MISSING FOREST

Overinterpretation and
Hyperliteralism

A person who is trying to understand a text is always projecting.

HANS-GEORG GADAMER

I have planted two churches in my lifetime, the first a congregation in the town of Twenty-nine Palms, California. I met many interesting people in that remote desert community—and I'm being generous when I say *interesting.* Some of these desert dwellers are trying to escape civilization, partly because no one in the civilized world appreciates their complex social, political, and religious machinations or the brilliance of their UFO theories—only they don't consider them theories. One "desert rat" I met was an old evangelist who had traveled the country with his wife, preaching in every little church that would host them.

I had a deep fondness for the Rev, and I loved his stories—especially the one in which he and his wife ran out of gas in the middle of nowhere, asked God for help, and watched in amazement as the needle on the gas gauge slowly rotated from E to F! But he did have a few strange ideas about God. One time we were talking about the Bible and the Holy Spirit—his favorite topics—and he explained that the Holy *Spirit* was not the same as the Holy *Ghost*. The latter terminology is found in the *King James Version*, the "authorized" version, according to the Rev.

Although I explained that both English words, *Spirit* and *Ghost*, translate the same Greek word, the Rev was neither impressed nor moved from his conviction. He was persuaded that the *King James Version* was as inspired as the biblical texts in the original languages. Therefore, he argued, God had a reason for differentiating between Spirit and Ghost. When I suggested that some of the language in the *King James* was archaic, and that I doubted that the Spirit of God appreciates being referred to as a ghost, he gave me a scowl and broke off our conversation.

The Rev had invented an aberrant doctrine based on a misinterpretation. No one could accuse him of minimizing what the Bible had to say about the Holy Spirit. As a matter of fact, his error was in the opposite direction: He made *too much* out of what the Bible said. This is a danger when interpreting the Bible. We can latch on to an insignificant point, and through overinterpretation and hyperliteralism we formulate a heretical doctrine.

Through the centuries, the Scriptures have been twisted, misunderstood, corrupted, and misinterpreted. Some misreadings are fairly innocent and don't result in severe distortions of truth. But other misreadings have given birth to heretical movements, cults, and deadly lies. Countless people have suffered oppression, abuse, and even torture at the hands of ardent Bible believers who were blind to their error. When people regard the Bible as God's sacred Word, it becomes incredibly dangerous when the text is misused. I would be doing you a great disservice if I failed to mention two errors that frequently result in misinterpretation: overinterpretation and hyperliteralism.[1]

Even though passages of Scripture may be open to several different interpretations, they are not open to any and all interpretation. Some interpretations must be rejected outright. There are external and internal constraints on the possible meaning of a biblical text. The internal constraints are found in the text itself, which will allow some interpretations but will exclude others. The external constraints include interpretive methods, tools, and skills like those covered in the previous chapters.

> ### THE BIG IDEA:
>
> Poor or improper interpretations of Scripture can be avoided if we are aware of approaches that tend to read too much into a text or extract more from a text than what is warranted.

If we are going to handle the Bible with integrity, we have to do our best to ensure that the meaning we find is really there and not a meaning we produced either by being too clever or simply by being mistaken. False doctrines do not usually originate outside the Bible but from a misreading of the Bible. If we understand clearly how believers go wrong and why they go wrong, we can be on guard against potential dangers of misinterpreting Scripture.

ZEALOUS TOWARD GOD:
OVERINTERPRETATION

To overinterpret a text is to draw unwarranted meanings from it; to place too much emphasis on the elements of words, grammar, and punctuation; to move beyond interpretation to invention by using details from a passage to launch into a separate universe of meaning. In short, overinterpretation involves making the text say more than it was meant to say and discovering meanings that simply are not there. The Bible was not written to be a mysterious book full of hidden and obscure meanings. To sift through it looking for secret encryption and then come up with something like a prediction of the assassination of Abraham Lincoln requires an extremely imaginative mind. Plus, in all cases of encoded predictions, the secret is "discovered" only *after* it's fulfilled.

I will briefly outline the most common causes of overinterpretation. Do not be surprised if you recognize some of these tendencies in your own

Bible study or in the teaching and preaching of someone you know. Over-interpretation is rampant among Christians.

Overinterpretation is often the result of *an exaggerated concept of inspiration.* There are people who believe the inspiration of Scripture extends not only to the original texts but even to the very words chosen in English translations (at least the *King James Version*). According to some fringe teachers, not only every word, but even the *letters* that make up the words of Scripture were purposefully chosen by God. This misconception is actually a continuation of a strain of rabbinical tradition that evolved into cabalism, where every little marking in Scripture was believed to have a secret, mystical meaning.

This exaggerated notion of inspiration has led to a fairly recent mis-use of Scripture that was published in the book *The Bible Code.*[2] Accord-ing to the book's author, the Bible contains encoded messages that can be revealed by isolating the letters that occur in particular mathematical sequences. With the help of computers, these hidden messages can be extracted from a large body of text. Besides the fact that the Bible itself gives no warrant for this type of analysis, *The Bible Code* has been widely criticized by theologians, mathematicians, and philologists.

One of the favorite amusements of the code's critics is to look for hid-den messages and predictions in *Moby Dick* using the Bible code method. So far they have found predictions of the assassinations of Indira Gandhi, Martin Luther King Jr., and John F. Kennedy, as well as Princess Diana's death and President George W. Bush's war on terrorism. This shows that any large body of text will yield any message a person is looking for if he has enough ingenuity.

I do not know of even one credible theologian who believes that the inspiration of Scripture includes such minutia as the choice of every letter that appears in the text. Jesus' comment regarding not "one jot or one tittle" passing away cannot be construed as an argument for inspiration since that was not His point (Matthew 5:18, KJV). Remember that portions of Scripture are quotations from pagans, Satan (see Matthew 4:2-10—the temptation of Christ), and those who mocked Jesus. If we were to find an inspired code in the letters of the words these people spoke, that would mean that God inspired the evil that came from their mouths. Even if we adopted the Jewish approach to a Bible code, which began by studying only the letters of words in the Torah, we still find instances of words spoken by the tempter to Eve, the rebellious Korah, and the blasphemies of Lamech and Pharaoh.

There is a fair amount of agreement among conservative theologians regarding the inspiration of Scripture, that it is both the Word of God and the word of humans, that the authors were not stenographers to whom God dictated His message word for word. In fact, each author had his own distinct style so that we can compare and contrast, for example, the style of Luke to that of John. Each scribe recorded God's inspired Word using his own personal style. Christians who look for encrypted messages in the Scriptures are treating the Bible as a magical book rather than revering it as the inspired Word of God.

An exaggerated notion of inspiration is common among many pastors who believe the only authentic way to teach the Bible is verse by verse. The idea here is that every verse of Scripture independently stands by itself as a revelation from God and, if mined for its treasures, will yield a truth or truths. I have heard renowned Bible teachers work their way through a passage, reading one verse at a time, then giving a short sermon that does nothing to explain the verse in its context. The verse is merely a pretext the preacher uses to deliver personal views and opinions, harangue his audience, or repeat the well-known themes evangelical Christians already believe.

If a verse-by-verse teacher responds that he is taking every verse in sequence and considering it in the light of the preceding verses, this is still insufficient. A complete unit of thought extends beyond any one verse and includes verses that follow as well as those that come before. Readers have to arrive at the end of the thought unit before they can know the meaning of the whole thought. Verses exist within even larger contexts— chapters, sections, books, Testaments, the whole Bible, history, culture, and so on. As we have seen, the whole explains the details, and the details give the sense of the whole.

The verse divisions used in English translations of the Bible were not original to the text or the author, so in the truest sense, verse-by-verse teaching is not biblical. In many cases, verse divisions are misleading or clearly misplaced. Perhaps a more accurate way to stay faithful to the meaning of the text would be a thought-by-thought study, taking into consideration the broad themes of a book before examining the details. At the same time, the details always need to be related to the whole.

Overinterpretation also occurs when people look for "secret wisdom" through some form of esoteric reading. These people are either skeptical of—or bored with—the meaning of Scripture that emerges through normal methods of interpretation. They have to apply ultraspiritual means of deciphering the Bible's contents. Sometimes a person will read the Bible one word at a time, looking up each word in a dictionary and spiritualizing what he finds. To study the Bible in this way gives the interpreter a sense of empowerment, as if he were led to a secret truth, a kind of cosmic key to unlock the mysteries of God. This sort of discovery is intoxicating, but it is also bogus.

People who overinterpret often overestimate the importance of details. There are Bible teachers who build entire ministries based on the Hebrew and Greek meanings of names and places or the etymologies of biblical words. How important is it that Elijah was a Tishbite or that some of the Levitical gatekeepers were stationed "At Parbar westward, four at the causeway, and two at Parbar" (1 Chronicles 26:18, KJV)? To overstate the significance of details such as these is to do a disservice to the overall meaning of a passage and thus to go astray.

Another sort of overinterpretation occurs when a person scrambles letters, words, or texts to produce new texts. Suppose I wanted to find the phrase "God is Jesus" in the Old Testament using the *New International Version*. In Genesis 1:1, I find the word *God*. In verse 28, I discover the letters *i-s* embedded in the word *fish* (an early Christian symbol). In Genesis 10:16, I come across the word *Jebusites,* and if I take a "bite" out of that word (b-i-t-e), the leftover letters can be arranged to spell the name *Jesus.* I now have the phrase I was looking for. This is a ridiculous example, of course, but it illustrates what Umberto Eco noted regarding this sort of overinterpretation, that "given the limited number of letters in the alphabet that a text combines, with such a method we could find any statement we wish in any text whatsoever."[3]

Another form of this error is sometimes referred to as *bibliomancy,* in which people use the Bible as if it were a divining instrument. This misapplication seeks to spell out answers to questions or discern divine guidance by turning pages at random and piecing together whatever words their eyes happen to land upon. No matter how unrelated those words or verses might be, our minds are agile enough to find messages and produce interpretations to *any* set of words or phrases.

Michael Gazzaniga, author of *The Social Brain,* theorized that the brain must have an "interpreter module" in the left dominant hemisphere of right-handed humans that produces interpretations for behavior that are otherwise detached from any conscious motivation. Research with "split-brain" patients showed that they could create rational explanations for their actions with one half of their brain that was unaware of the motivation of the other half because the hemispheres had been surgically separated.[4]

Stanley Fish, chairman of the Department of English at Duke University, writes in his book *Is There a Text in This Class?* about a less-sophisticated but equally fascinating experiment conducted with students in two successive classes. He wrote the following names of four linguists and a literary critic on the chalkboard:

Jacobs—Rosenbaum

Levin

Thorne

Hayes

Ohman (?)

Fish then told his class that these words formed a religious poem and their job was to interpret it. What is amazing is the profound and intricate interpretations the students were able to spontaneously produce.[5] The fact that we can find associations between words randomly extracted from the text does not mean that we have discovered a secret message, but rather that we possess a God-given ability to produce rational associations for items and ideas that have no rational connection.

Another form of overinterpretation results from linking Scripture to conspiracy theories. People who believe in UFOs, world-domination threats from secret societies, or government plots to control the thinking of its citizens by putting chemicals into water supplies often point to Bible passages to document their theories. For some reason they feel this gives their elaborate scenarios more credibility. But as we saw before, if you go to the Bible with an idea that you want to prove, you can make the Bible say anything. When interpreting a passage, we must keep in mind the major themes of the Bible: the sinfulness of human nature, the need for redemption, the history of salvation culminating in the death and resurrection of Jesus Christ, and the promise of a transformed life in the present and eternal life with God when we have finished our course here.

In his book *Conspiracy,* Daniel Pipes demonstrates how conspiracy theories are inspired and driven by fear. Behind every conspiracy theory is what he terms the "paranoid style."[6] With this in mind, we need to be wary of people who see universal threats or cover-ups, because these sensationalized "revelations" not only create undue alarm, they take our eyes off what should be our real concern. I cannot help but think of God's word to His prophet Isaiah:

> The LORD spoke to me with his strong hand upon me, warning me not to follow the way of this people. He said:
>
> "Do not call conspiracy
>   everything that these people call conspiracy;

do not fear what they fear,
    and do not dread it.
The LORD Almighty is the one you are to regard as holy,
    he is the one you are to fear,
    he is the one you are to dread,
and he will be a sanctuary." (Isaiah 8:11-14)

Overinterpretation can also result from making too much of coincidence or irrelevant similarities that exist between two separate ideas, objects, or themes. There are people who will find descriptions of advanced weapons of war in Scripture. Because a chariot was a war vehicle, it is in this regard similar to an armored tank, but does that similarity justify interpreting chariots as tanks in the prophetic books of the Bible? That association can be made only if someone is really straining.

Associations often are made between two items because they are similar in the way they function, belong to the same class of things (for instance, plants, weapons, or commodities), share a similar form (the letter "t" has the shape of a cross), or appear together in some other context. But similarities between things do not mean they share a true relationship or that the one always implies the other.

One of the most beloved passages in the Bible is Isaiah 40:30-31:

Even youths grow tired and weary,
    and young men stumble and fall;
but those who hope in the LORD
    will renew their strength.
They will soar on wings like eagles;
    they will run and not grow weary,
    they will walk and not be faint.

The metaphor of soaring on wings of eagles is both lovely and encouraging, but to go beyond the metaphor is to overinterpret.

Suppose a Bible student draws the conclusion that believers who hope in (or "wait on") the Lord are like eagles. The student then turns to an encyclopedia and discovers all kinds of interesting information about eagles—where and how high they build their nests, the coloration of their plumage, their monogamous pairing, the range of their hunting in relationship to their nests, their wingspan, diet, and so on. Then the student finds (invents) spiritual attributes for all these bits of data. Even though he may have produced a very interesting and devotional thesis, the meaning of the text has not been made clearer, but just the opposite: It has been obscured. The problem with overinterpretation is that it resists the most apparent meaning of the text in its attempt to find mystical or more spiritual meanings.

Sometimes, after researching a subject and finding analogies from eagles (or sheep, morning dew, grapevines) that can be applied to the spiritual life of a believer, the student resists the idea that these associations were not intended by either Isaiah or God. In fact, the student is convinced that he was led by God to these "revelations" and they are *true*. The question, however, is whether the student has discovered the meaning of the text or used the text to invent something else.

Umberto Eco argues that, in everyday life, humans distinguish relevant and significant similarities from illusory or coincidental similarities. He gives an example in which we see someone from a distance and mistake him for someone we know, but after observing him more closely, realize he is a stranger.[7] Perhaps you have made the embarrassing mistake—as I have—of calling out a friend's name to someone who turned out to be a stranger. Now how much more ridiculous would it be to approach that person and *insist* that he was not who he thought he was but was actually your friend? We do that very thing with biblical texts if we insist that their meaning is what we have produced through overinterpretation.

When a Bible teacher attaches a prophecy from Scripture to a current event and insists that what we see in the news is the fulfillment of that biblical prediction, he is overinterpreting. In spite of the fact that the European Economic Community (EEC) now consists of more than ten nations, there are advocates of end-times teaching who will not give up the idea that the EEC is the fulfillment of the ten-toed kingdom of Nebuchadnezzar's dream in the book of Daniel. Likewise, there are those who continue to insist that Russia is the northern threat that will descend on Israel in the battle of Ezekiel 38, even though the Soviet Union has collapsed and the ancient kingdoms mentioned in Ezekiel are outside the borders of Russia (Meshech and Tubal are known to have been in central and eastern Anatolia, present-day Turkey).[8]

If we go to the Bible looking for mystical enlightenment or the secrets of the ages—as do many cults—then we have already abandoned the purpose the Bible establishes for itself. If we read Scripture with an open mind and an open heart to discover what is there, we will find a history of God and His people with important revelations about His nature, covenants, and activity in the world. The Bible in its entirety leads us to the hope of forgiveness, relationship with God and others, personal transformation, and eternal life through the death and resurrection of Jesus Christ. If we long for something more sublime, esoteric, or exotic, then we are likely to bring an attitude to the Scriptures that will cause us to overinterpret what is there and miss the real point of God's Word.

FROM COVER TO COVER: HYPERLITERALISM

I was once in a church where a preacher lifted his oversize Bible and, shaking it back and forth, declared, "I believe the Bible from cover to cover... and I even believe the cover, because it says, 'Holy Bible!'" Such a bold assertion of confidence in the Bible is commendable. We must be convinced of the Bible's truth and reliability if we are going to let it be our guide. But belief is something we need to guard so that it does not degrade into gullibility or fideism.[9]

Hyperliteralism is at the opposite end of the spectrum from doubt. If doubt is believing too little, hyperliteralism is believing too much. When the Jews misunderstood Jesus' words about destroying the temple, or Nicodemus questioned whether he had to reenter the womb to be born again, they were being hyperliteral. The problem of hyperliteralism is that people will read a passage in such a way that the text is not allowed to speak for itself. Instead, the text is forced into a style dictated by the reader. Hyperliteralism produces false meanings because the text is weakened by being read in a context other than its own.

The Enlightenment, a philosophical movement during the eighteenth century, probably had something to do with this error. In their demand for a rational explanation for every idea and belief, Enlightenment philosophers created a new tension for Christian faith. In order to accommodate biblical belief to that kind of rationalism, Christians began to treat the Bible as if it could be read like a philosophical or scientific textbook.

Perhaps because science was growing in prestige at the beginning of the twentieth century, conservative Christians felt they had to prove that the literal text of the Bible was in agreement with archaeological and historical records as well as the findings of science. Since Christians were biased in favor of the Bible, any conflicts between a literal reading of Scripture and scientific claims meant that science was in error. The motto of the hyperliteralists has been "Let God be true, but every man a liar" (Romans 3:4, KJV).

The problem is that once believers began to stress the literal interpretation of Scripture, they did not always know when to stop. Critics of Christianity took advantage of this and began to press believers on issues that were either specious or silly. Some Christians found themselves defending literal interpretations of passages that were not meant to be taken literally. They did the best they could to provide logically sound arguments for their hyperliteral interpretations.

Hyperliteralism is an attempt to be true to the biblical text, which is a good thing. The problem stems from the fact that hyperliteralism *alters* the text. It is not hyperliteralism to believe God struck Egypt with a series of plagues, that Samson was given superhuman strength, or that Peter walked on water. All of those stories were meant to be understood as actual events. But there are portions of Scripture that were not meant to be interpreted literally, such as the use of hyperbole in the book of Revelation.

Correct interpretation requires that we understand Scripture within the literary style and according to the devices employed by the writer. We slip into hyperliteralism when we refuse to read figurative or metaphorical passages according to their literary style. For example, there is a prophetic passage having to do with an event that is supposed to take place in the Jezreel Valley near the historic hilltop city of Megiddo—the end-times conflagration known as the Battle of Armageddon. Many who teach biblical prophecy claim that the carnage of that battle is depicted in Revelation 14:20: "They were trampled in the winepress outside the city, and blood flowed out of the press, rising as high as the horses' bridles for a distance of 1,600 stadia" (or nearly two hundred miles). I have heard people claim that the Jezreel Valley will be literally filled with blood up to approximately five feet.

This is an example of hyperliteralism in which the interpreters are unable to recognize hyperbole, a figure of speech in which exaggerations are used for an effect. It is not a question of whether such a thing could happen or even if our imaginations are supposed to be stretched by the enormity of the bloodbath, but it is a question of how we are supposed to interpret this statement. If the amount of blood to be spilt is meant to be taken literally, then why do these same interpreters not also teach that a giant winepress did in fact lay "outside the city"? Oddly, they can recognize one figure of speech (metaphor) but not another (hyperbole).

Another related instance of hyperliteralism appears when people look at current events for literal applications of obscure prophecies. There has been no end of speculation regarding the "mark of the beast" and the devious utilization of the number 666 in tattoos, computer chips embedded under the skin, and so on. There are people so convinced that the fulfillment of this prophecy is on the horizon that they are leery of credit cards or any universal forms of identification (although the latter fear is probably moot given our current understanding of DNA).

Unfortunately, Christians are made to feel paranoid regarding technological advances in credit and ID that have nothing to do with the radical turmoil spoken of in Revelation. They fear the "beast" is sneaking up on them, when the story in Revelation 13 is anything but a surprise attack. The answer to the question "How will we know when this is happening?" is "You will know!"

Another regrettable effect of hyperliteralism is the inability to distinguish between Christian and Jewish cultures, customs, and commands. Paul fought a continual battle to prevent Christianity from becoming a Jewish cult. His contention with the party of strict Jews who wanted to enforce their regulations on Gentiles took him all the way to the highest authorities in the Christian church (see Acts 15). It was there decided that Gentiles did not first have to become Jews in order to become Christians. Nevertheless, there were still people—and there still *are* people—who insist that Christians must keep the Sabbath according to Old Testament law. In fact, there are Christians who are more Old Testament in their mentality than they are New Testament. They are still trying to establish their own righteousness through their own good works (see Romans 10:1-3).

Hyperliteralism also prevails when no allowances are made for changes in historical or cultural conditions. When Paul wrote to the Corinthians and said a woman should wear a veil over her head when prophesying in public, he was concerned with modesty and how Christian women would be perceived if they disregarded a cultural norm. Unveiled women in Corinth—which is the same even today in strict Islamic cultures—were considered immoral. But there are many cultures now in which this tradition is irrelevant. To continue to enforce the rule of the veil in cultures where veils are never worn misses a larger point. To apply standards of modest attire in Christian community is a literal and reasonable application of the text, but to require women to wear veils in church is a hyperliteral application. Sadly, there are cases in which Christians pursuing holiness have merely achieved weirdness.

A Word of Encouragement

The Bible is the authoritative foundation for Christian theology and faith, but there are many practical and very personal uses for the Bible as well. The text confronts us and makes us aware of personal sin and wrongdoing (see 2 Timothy 3:16), but it also builds endurance, encouragement, and hope (see Romans 15:4). There is a way to read the Bible in which every word feels like a personal attack and a reminder of all that you are doing wrong, and there is a way of reading the Bible in which every word is a revelation of what God wants to do in your life to energize your spirit and fill you with joy. An honest reading of the Bible will do both: break you down at times and build you up at other times, "rebuke" and "correct" (see Jeremiah 1:10; 2 Timothy 3:16). My concern is that you do not get stuck in the "break down" mode and never find your soul refreshed and encouraged by God through His Word.

My desire is for you to be able to see deeper into the truth of God's Word, feel a greater passion for discovering its meaning, commit yourself to its commands, and live closer to God by learning to hear His voice. Now it is time for you to put *this* book down, pick up your Bible, and let God speak to you. May it please the Lord our God to give you eyes to see, ears to hear, and a heart to perceive what He is revealing in the Scriptures.

THE SOURCE OF
AUTHORITY

Why We Need to Practice the
Skills of Interpretation

Thirty years ago, when my dad's church in Southern California was attracting thousands of hippies, people would regularly drop by our home looking for spiritual help or perhaps a handout. One day a very upset young woman showed up. (I'll refer to her as Minnie.) Since no one else was home, she asked if she could talk to me. I was a rascally seventeen-year-old preacher's kid, but I had enough sense to see she was desperate, so we talked.

Minnie had a soft voice, and several times I had to ask her to speak up. If her caricature were drawn as a cartoon animal, she would have been a mouse—not Mickey; she lacked his spunk. She leaned forward and kept her arms bent next to her body. She trembled slightly as she spoke.

Minnie had been living in a Christian commune governed by a group of legalistic "elders." These leaders attempted to recreate the environment described in the first four chapters of Acts, where believers shared every-thing in common and frequently ate together. If these hippie-Christians had formerly lived freewheeling lives unrestrained by rules, they now swung to the opposite extreme, creating a prisonlike compound.

The wives were basically told not to think and were treated as slaves.

The logic the men used to keep their wives in submission (actually, servitude) relied on two assumptions. First, they pointed to the story of the Fall in Genesis 3. Eve was said to be at fault because she was the first to disobey God. They acknowledged that Adam also ate the fruit, but his sin was given a heroic twist—he felt obligated to join his wife. (One can almost hear Ricky Ricardo saying, "Ohhhhh Lucy! What haf you dun now?")

Second, they jumped to the New Testament to explain *why* Eve fell to the serpent's temptation: She was "deceived" (see 1 Timothy 2:14). And why was she deceived? The answer required more page turning, to 1 Corinthians 11 where Paul said, "The head of the woman is man" (verse 3). Eve was deceived because Adam wasn't with her; she was "without her head." Well, of course! If you go around without your head, you're going to be deceived by even amateur con artists.

The implications of this logic were spelled out in the roles husbands and wives were to play in marriage. If the man is "the head," then he does all the thinking. If a wife goes anywhere without her husband, she is without her head and therefore without her brains. So wives had to submit to their husbands in every decision. To cap off this interpretive sleight of hand, women were reminded that the Bible enjoins wives to "submit" to their husbands (Ephesians 5:22). Since the elders of this commune linked the word "submit" to the "head" passage in 1 Corinthians, they drew the conclusion that wives were to defer *all* thinking to their husbands.

Minnie was suffering from spiritual and emotional abuse. If she made any attempt to question the elders' teaching, she was told that the devil would deceive her if she didn't submit to their authority. Further, they said, God would desert her if she left the fold. She asked me if the Bible really taught that women must not think for themselves.

Anyone with even the most rudimentary skills in biblical interpretation could dismantle the false teaching of her commune—a good thing since my skills were minimal. But their argument seemed convincing for a new Christian. After all, she had learned her "proper place" as a woman in a Bible study, and the leaders were Christians who could quote a lot of verses to prove their case.

> ### THE BIG IDEA:
>
> A "good Bible study" is not a collection of Bible verses, but the careful analysis of one passage. If a teacher doesn't acknowledge that he is *interpreting* the Bible, then his words wrongly assume the full force of biblical authority.

What difference does it make if we know something about history, culture, original language, or various ways of reading and understanding a text? Can't we simply read our English translations and find everything God intended us to learn? Almost every major Bible scholar and teacher—from the first century to the present—has emphasized the importance of having a basic knowledge and skill for correctly interpreting the Bible, without which we are liable to misread and misinterpret Scripture. It's essential that we learn and practice the skills of biblical interpretation.

SHAKY STRUCTURES

At the conclusion of the Sermon on the Mount, Jesus ended with a story about two builders. One of them built a house on bedrock, the other built on sand. Both houses were beaten by a severe storm and flood, but only the house on bedrock stood. In this parable Jesus brought home the lesson, that "everyone who hears these words of mine and puts them into practice is like a wise man who built his house on the rock" (Matthew 7:24).

Teaching a Bible lesson is like building a house. Teachers construct mental frameworks that shape our thinking about God and our lives in the world. The framework can be built on an authentic and solid foundation or it can be built on sand. The leaders of Minnie's commune built their house on sand. By isolating passages, verses, and even words from their contexts and giving them their own definitions, they constructed a spiritual house that was dangerous for anyone who tried to live in it.

Cults create heretical worldviews in the same way. They construct models of reality using the teachings of various prophets and enlightened masters, sometimes even throwing in a smattering of pseudoscience, borrowing the credibility of physics or biology. People who join cults are eventually brainwashed into a worldview, and that is one of the hooks that makes leaving a cult so difficult. Bible cults are especially difficult to leave, because people who escape them still hear the wacky lessons replayed in their mind whenever they try to read the Bible.

Without creating a cult, many Christians have also constructed shaky frameworks. They run hither, thither, and yon throughout the Bible as they present verse after verse to prove their case. If they talk fast enough or if their credentials seem solid, it can be hard to resist their logic. But their frameworks can be taken apart and shown to be nothing but the invention of an overactive imagination.

BELIEF SYSTEMS

Every belief system is man-made, since a belief system is the mental framework people construct out of a collection of beliefs. Belief systems embody the essential assumptions (or presuppositions) a community holds regarding the world, their place in it, and their relationship to others. A doctrinal statement or creed is a codified belief system. Some belief systems are closer to the truth of Scripture than others. Every belief system should be subjected to strident criticism, and if found false, then dismantled. If we learn how to determine when a verse is properly used and ask whether a word means what someone says it means, then we can evaluate the validity and truth of a belief system.

Preachers or students of the Bible can get excited about what looks like a fascinating, profound, or mysterious new revelation. Sometimes they think they have found the secret of a perfect marriage or a sinless life or harnessing the superpower of the Holy Spirit. They piece together scattered Bible verses and link them to build their case. However, what holds those unrelated verses together is not their content, but the framework designed by the clever preacher.

We can compare this type of a belief system (mental framework) to a Christmas tree. Over the years you have collected different ornaments. Some are colorful and festive and have secular themes: Santa Claus, toys, and wreaths. Others have religious themes relating to Christ's birth. And others have traditional or commercial themes with no particular reference to Christmas—for example, a cartoon character like Garfield the cat. What relationship do these ornaments have to each other? None, except that they all hang on the same tree. If the only thing that links two verses together is the coincidence that they were both pulled from the Bible, then those verses are being misused.

Along these lines, cross references in the margins of our Bibles cannot always be trusted. Often, when you read one verse and find a reference to another, the only thing they have in common is the accident of sharing one English word. The subject or meaning of the two verses may not be related at all. Neither is it wise to take a particular word and collect all the verses in which that word appears to build a theology around it. Theologians have provided us an indispensable service by establishing boundaries and guidelines that govern the relationship of one verse or passage to another.

Learning to interpret passages within their own contexts will protect us from creating defective belief systems. We will find the subject or message of a passage and then be able to compare it to the message of other passages. When we make an exciting discovery—and there will be many—we will have our hands on something that is really there, something God intended us to find.

POWER TO THE PREACHER

The Scriptures provide us with our only reliable guide to God's self-revelation and His will regarding our lives. The deep reverence that we have for Scripture precludes us from contradicting its teaching or rejecting its truth. We accept its authority.

However, most people who read the Bible are like the Ethiopian eunuch in Acts 8. He was reading in the prophecy of Isaiah when Philip asked him, "Do you understand what you are reading?" The eunuch answered, "How can I…unless someone explains it to me?" (Acts 8:30-31). At some point, everyone who has tried to understand the Bible has needed someone else to explain it to them. But to allow someone to tell you what the Bible means involves a built-in vulnerability: Students have to submit to their teacher's superior knowledge in order to learn from them.

At this point we should begin to feel a bit nervous. If the Bible is the authoritative Word of God, and a human stands between you and the Bible to explain it to you, then the authority of the Bible, at least for a moment, rests with the interpreter. In other words, the authority of the Bible is transferred to the person who tells me what the Bible means. There are problems with this arrangement. First, it is not always understood that we have yielded this authority to the interpreter or preacher—and very subtly that person has come to stand in the place of God. Second, preachers often deny they have any such authority and also deny that they interpret the Bible. You may have even heard a preacher say, "Don't get mad at me, folks, this isn't my opinion; it's right there in the Word of God! If you don't like it, don't argue with me; argue with God."

Do you see how dangerous this logic can be? Preachers who make these statements act as the mouthpiece of God, yet deny that they are doing so. They can present themselves as humble yet righteous at the same time when they give the disclaimer, "I am not interpreting the Bible, just quoting it." However, they fail to mention that they had first created a context for the verses they quote, and the context strongly influences the way those verses will be understood. The truth is, even to *read* a text involves interpretation.

If anyone suggests or implies (even by quoting a verse as a proof text) *any* meaning for any particular verse, that person is interpreting. Interpreting a passage is not a sin, rather a necessity. What is wrong is failing to admit that we are engaging in interpretation and that our interpretations are always open to question. The problem intensifies in churches and institutions—for instance, private schools—that are admittedly authoritarian in their corporate, social, or political structure. If anyone teaching the Bible argues that he is not interpreting the Bible, then that person's words assume the full force of biblical authority—an authority that is both binding and divine.

To invest God's authority in a human interpreter is a severe mistake when the preacher is unscrupulous, but it is also a serious problem even when the preacher is trying hard to please God. The preacher's interpretation of a text can be mistaken for "God's truth." Perhaps the leaders in Minnie's commune, referred to at the beginning of this chapter, really did believe that women are intellectually inferior to men. Maybe they thought they were reading the plain words of Scripture and would have denied that they had added their own interpretation. But good intentions notwithstanding, they still did a lot of damage to the people under their care, and they mishandled the Bible.

We can protect ourselves from placing excessive confidence in preachers and interpreters by becoming careful interpreters ourselves through faithful study and reliance on the Holy Spirit as our teacher. As skilled interpreters, we can develop a reasonable skepticism regarding the interpretations of others (see 1 Thessalonians 5:19-22). We can also evaluate their interpretations to determine how biblical, rational, and edifying they are.

The Bible is inspired, but our interpretations are not. Our interpretations can be improved, modified, even replaced as our knowledge and interpretive skill increase. Interpreters can be wrong, misguided, confused, and uninformed. Therefore nothing that anyone says about the Bible is equal to the authority of the Bible.

If you hear a preacher or Bible teacher say something that disturbs you, sounds odd, or seems manipulative or controlling, do not blindly accept the lesson. Take your concern to other trusted friends, scholars, and spiritual leaders as well as conducting your own study. Do not submit yourself to the authority of a teacher (other than the Holy Spirit) with the same deference that you give to the Scriptures.

INTERPRETATION OR MANIPULATION?

There is another, very sad, issue we need to look into, and that is the case of Bible teachers using Scripture to manipulate people. Some of the most popular and widely promoted church programs are designed to control potential church members. In order to ensure the continued attendance of first-time visitors, for instance, churches will immediately introduce them to the new members' class. Eventually, the new member will be given a volunteer position that will embed him or her in the life of the institution. In most cases, greater involvement in the church is equated with spiritual growth in Christ.

I don't question the importance of the church as a spiritual community. We need the mutual support, encouragement, and prodding that comes through close relationships with other believers. We need the synergy that comes through combining strengths, gifts, and resources. We need the spiritual environment that occurs in communal worship. But we should stop and ask, Am I being incorporated into a religious organization, or am I being trained and nurtured to know God through Jesus Christ? Many churches look and function like large businesses, and the ideal member is a contributor, client, and salary-free employee.

Preachers often feel compelled—wrongly—to demonstrate how building and supporting the institution of the church is identical to obeying

God's Word. Therefore, when the announcement is made that volunteers are needed for the nursery, it is preceded with a Bible verse and maybe even a brief sermon. When the offering is taken, church members are reminded of a number of biblical texts regarding giving, such as, "God loveth a cheerful giver" (2 Corinthians 9:7, KJV). Therefore, financial support for this particular institution is advertised as a believer's biblical duty.

How is an insecure minister going to prevent people from leaving his church to visit or join other congregations—especially when there are so many glitzy churches popping up all over town? It seems to me that Jesus always gave people the option to leave Him and even asked the Twelve whether they were going to stay (see John 6:66-67). But He is the exception. Other ministers feel it is necessary to control the movements (and thinking) of their members.

The strategy of some ministers—although never articulated in quite this way—is first to convince church members that theirs is the only church in the community preaching the complete truth of God's Word. (There are ministers who will go so far as to suggest that even reading the literature published by other churches or denominations can turn a person's thoughts away from the truth. In the 1970s I met Christians in Sweden who weren't allowed to read Francis Schaeffer's writings because he wasn't Pentecostal.) Then it is implied that a person can't be a mature Christian if he embraces the corrupted faith of another church. Thus people are guaranteed that they will receive the truth and enjoy a good standing with God *if they stay put.*

Think about this next assertion: "If you *really* loved God, then you would want to serve the children in our nursery." Have you ever heard a preacher speak those words? They can be used for any endeavor, from supporting missionaries to serving as a camp counselor. There are people who can't see through this crude manipulative tactic. They trust their minister as interpreter of the Bible, so they accept the implications of the pastor's teaching. If a church member dares to question the teaching of an authoritarian pastor, he is led to the verses of Scripture that tell Christians to respect, obey, and submit to their spiritual leaders.

We can only challenge another person's use or misuse of the Bible if we ourselves have some level of competence in biblical interpretation. Otherwise, we are at the mercy of those who appear to be the experts.

In the New Testament, the Berean Christians were commended for checking on their teachers and questioning their interpretation of Scripture. "Now the Bereans were of more noble character than the Thessalonians, for they received the message with great eagerness and examined the Scriptures every day to see if what Paul said was true" (Acts 17:11). By the way, you might want to test my application of this text in Acts with your own reading and interpretation.

HARD SAYINGS

A number of passages in Scripture are notoriously difficult to interpret. Either the wording of the original language is strange, or a sentence seems misplaced, or the meaning of a verse is simply hard to take at face value. I don't believe any interpretive method is going to dissolve all the difficulties, and I am certain there are some things God means for us to only partially understand. Nevertheless, having access to a variety of interpretive methods will help us unlock the meaning of some texts that at first are either troubling or confusing.

I once read that the reason creative people don't get stuck when trying to solve a problem is because they are able to change their field of reference. They can look at problems from different points of view or in a different context. Suppose you are reading in 1 Samuel and come to the place where God told Samuel to anoint David as Israel's next king. Since King Saul was still alive, Samuel protested that he could lose his head if Saul found out about David. God told Samuel to take a cow with him and tell the people of Bethlehem that he had come to offer sacrifice to God.

Was God telling Samuel to lie? If so, then what does that say about the character of God? Some people might get "stuck" at this point, thinking, *No matter how I interpret this passage, I cannot deny that God told Samuel to misrepresent his actions.* A creative person, however, might say, "I wonder what would happen if I read this passage in a different light? What if this were a chess match, a battlefield, a secret council?"

We often read the stories of the Bible as if they were meant to reveal a spiritual truth at every turn. But much of what we read is the depiction of actual human predicaments. Sometimes God is directly involved in those predicaments, and sometimes they just play out the way we would expect in normal life.

Suppose we read the above story again, but like a spy novel or an episode of *Mission Impossible.* "Samuel, this is your assignment if you choose to accept it." From the outset, Samuel is deployed on a covert operation. Of course he isn't going to divulge his secret mission. To avoid detection, he diverts attention from his main mission while he completes the assignment God gave him. There was no lie, but a necessary ruse, a secret strategy. A clandestine operation is exactly the sort of plot we would expect to find in the story of a king and his court. To know that God is the instigator of this secret mission serves to reassure us of David's calling and the fact that he will become king in spite of all the dangers he will encounter. (This is just one way to look at the story through a different lens.)

I can't read a book or magazine without reading glasses. But since I had perfect vision for most of my life, I usually live in denial and leave my glasses at home. Then, if my wife, Barbara, and I have dinner in a restaurant, I have to ask her to read the menu to me. When I finally realized I was going to either have to buy a large-print Bible or get some bifocals, I broke down and went to an optometrist.

When you have your eyes examined, the doctor swings a strange contraption in front of your face. A number of lenses are rotated in front of each eye, and you are asked to read the letters on a chart. Through some lenses, the letters look like fuzzy squiggles. Other lenses make the letters look only slightly blurred. But there will be one lens through which the letters are perfectly clear.

Interpretive methods work in a similar fashion. If you are reading a passage and the meaning seems blurry no matter how hard you try to make sense out of it, then you may need to use a different lens. Try a different method of interpretation, and suddenly a meaning comes into focus that you had not seen before.

Applying an interpretive method that draws a meaning to the surface of a verse is a lot like solving a puzzle. The same kind of mental work goes on: looking at the clues, determining what fits and what is important, making associations between pieces, and so on. But when the meaning rises from the text, the elation is even greater than when you solve a puzzle, because you have discovered a truth and God is speaking to you through that truth.

As you continue to study the Bible, use the tools of interpretation well and listen carefully for God to speak. You will see the meaning of Scripture open up to you as never before. You will receive God's grace. You will witness His will unfolding in your life with greater clarity. And you will recognize applications to your life that you've long been seeking.

"Let the word of Christ dwell in you richly as you teach and admonish one another with all wisdom, and as you sing psalms, hymns and spiritual songs with gratitude in your hearts to God" (Colossians 3:16). Amen.

NOTES

INTRODUCTION

1. Bernard Ramm, *Protestant Biblical Interpretation* (Grand Rapids, Mich.: Baker, 1978), 11.

2. Peter Harrison has advanced a competing theory in his book *The Bible, Protestantism, and the Rise of Natural Science*. Harrison argues that modern science did not give rise to new forms of interpretation, but the Reformers' new forms of interpretation provided science with a new way of interpreting the world of nature, which helped produce and shape the scientific method. Either way, biblical interpretation in the modern era was tethered to the scientific enterprise.

3. See Thomas Oden, ed., *The Ancient Christian Commentary on Scripture* (Downers Grove, Ill.: InterVarsity, 2002).

CHAPTER 1

1. Taken from James McAuley, *An Art of Poetry*. Reproduced by arrangement with the copyright owner, Norma McAuley in care of Curtis Brown (Aust) Pty Ltd.

2. For an example of this, see the expression "children of Belial" in Deuteronomy 13:13 and 1 Samuel 10:27 (KJV), where such people are not the literal offspring of Belial, but obnoxious troublemakers.

3. Overinterpretation refers to reading more into a text than is really there. The interpretation derived in this manner tends to be disconnected from the text's literal meaning. For more on this idea see chapter 10, "The Missing Forest."

CHAPTER 2

1. For more on this idea, see Claus Westermann, *Praise and Lament in the Psalms* (Atlanta: John Knox, 1981), 52-151.
2. Attributed to Roman Jakobson. Quoted in Terry Eagleton, *Literary Theory: An Introduction* (Minneapolis: University of Minnesota Press, 1996), 2.

CHAPTER 3

1. For examples of this, see Judges 9:7-15; 2 Samuel 12:1-4; Ezekiel 17:2-10.
2. See Ruth 1:6 in the *New International Version,* which translates *lachem* as "food."

CHAPTER 4

1. *The Matrix,* written and directed by Andy Wachowski and Larry Wachowski. Released by Warner Bros. in 1999.
2. The recurrence of the number seven draws attention to itself in the first chapter of Esther. The banquet lasted seven days (1:5,10), the king sent seven eunuchs to conduct the queen to the banquet hall (1:10), and he sought the counsel of seven advisors (1:14). Thus, there are three sets of sevens. Both *three* and *seven* are complete numbers and may have been emphasized to indicate that the king's great wealth was complete or as full as it could possibly be.
3. For instance, see the story of Deborah in Judges 4–5.

CHAPTER 5

1. Go to www.baldman.com for more on the feelings and experiences of the bald.

CHAPTER 6

1. For more on the dangers of overinterpretation, see chapter 10, "The Missing Forest."

CHAPTER 7

1. This view was advanced by nineteenth-century theologian Bruno Bauer, among others.

2. The majority of Christians who do not have an extensive education in biblical history will rely on commentaries, Bible dictionaries, and encyclopedias for much-needed help. There are also many popular reference works from which a wealth of material can be gleaned. Also, magazines such as *Biblical Archaeology Review* keep readers up to date on some of the most recent digs and discoveries in the Holy Land.

3. In order to research this passage of Scripture, I have conducted interviews, visited libraries at Bible colleges, and read a number of books and essays. Although you may not be interested in going to the same depth, and you might not have access to the extensive background resources that I have drawn from, this chapter will illustrate the basic process taken in historical research.

4. I want to express my deep gratitude to John Hallowell, who first introduced me to the historical data behind 1 Timothy 2. John delivered a paper to the 1989 American Academy of Religion/Society of Biblical Literature entitled "Feminine Vengeance and the Cult of Artemis," in which he explored the mythic and cultural use of the Greek word *authenteo*—a keyword in the translation and interpretation of the 1 Timothy passage. However, any mistakes in my analysis are my own.

5. If you're interested in doing further research into the particular religious climate in which Timothy was ministering, here are several valuable reference works that you'll find to be helpful:

Dieter Kinbbe, "Via Sacra Ephesiaca: New Aspects of the Cult of Artemis," in *Ephesos Metropolis of Asia: An Interdisciplinary Approach to Its Archeology, Religion, and Culture,* ed. Helmut Koester (Valley Forge, Pa.: Trinity Press International, 1995).

Richard Oster, *The Acts of the Apostles Part II* (Abilene, Tex.: Abilene Christian University Press, 1984).

Richard Oster, "The Ephesian Artemis As an Opponent of Early Christianity," *Jahrbruch für Antike und Christentum* (Jahrgang 19, 1976).

Leland Edward Wilshire, "The TLG Computer and Further Reference to *Authenteo* in 1 Timothy 2.12," *New Testament Studies* 34 (1988): 120134.

CHAPTER 8

1. Tom Terrific's dog was Mighty Manfred the Wonder Dog.
2. Walter Brueggemann, *Finally Comes the Poet: Daring Speech for Proclamation* (Minneapolis: Fortress, 1989), 115. See his chapter "Resistance and Relinquishment" for another example of a postcolonial interpretation of Daniel, especially pages 111-42.
3. Brueggemann, *Finally Comes the Poet*, 117.

CHAPTER 9

1. Guigo II, *The Ladder of Monks and Twelve Meditations*, trans. Edmund Colledge and James Walsh (Garden City, N.Y.: Doubleday Image, 1978; reprinted Kalamazoo, Mich.: Cistercian Publications, 1981). Found at http://www.umilta.net/ladder.html.
2. Guigo II, *The Ladder of Monks and Twelve Meditations*.
3. Guigo II, *The Ladder of Monks and Twelve Meditations*.

CHAPTER 10

1. This discussion addresses ways believers distort God's truth through misapplied interpretation. If, however, you are also concerned about the ways that non-Christians misuse the Bible, I recommend James Sire's *Scripture Twisting: 20 Ways the Cults Misread the Bible* (Downers Grove, Ill.: InterVarsity, 1980).
2. Michael Drosnin, *The Bible Code* (New York: Simon and Schuster, 1997).
3. Umberto Eco et al., "Overinterpreting Texts," in *Interpretation and Overinterpretation* (New York: Cambridge University Press, 1996), 57.

4. See Michael Gazzaniga, *The Social Brain: Discovering the Networks of the Mind* (New York: Basic Books, 1985), 70-75.

5. See Stanley Fish, "How to Recognize a Poem When You See One," *Is There a Text in This Class?: The Authority of Interpretive Communities* (Cambridge, Mass.: Harvard University Press, 1998), 322-37.

6. Daniel Pipes, *Conspiracy* (New York: Simon & Schuster, 1997), 22.

7. See Eco, *Interpretation and Overinterpretation*, 48.

8. See Edwin Yamauchi, "A Russian Invasion of Iran?" in *Foes from the Northern Frontier: Invading Hordes from the Russian Steppes* (Grand Rapids, Mich.: Baker, 1982), 19-27.

9. Fideism is an irrational commitment to a faith that is based on experience, because it is assumed that reason cannot provide a basis for faith or prove religious statements to be true.